Liverpool All-Time Greats

Anfield's finest players profiled

Liverpool
All-Time
Greats

Anfield's finest players profiled

§
SIENA

Siena
PO Box 14840
London NW3 5WT

ISBN 0-75252-375-9

Contents

Introduction

Though many can claim to have existed for a similar length of time, few football clubs can boast a fraction of the prestige, mystique and magic that surrounds the name of Liverpool FC. Merseyside, along with Glasgow and Manchester, has traditionally been one of the hotbeds of what has, until recently, been a working-class game.

RELIGION

Scousers live, breathe and sleep football, while their heroes are worshipped like no others. 'What will you do when Christ comes to Merseyside?' ran a banner outside a local church in the 1960s. The felt-tipped response, 'Move St John to inside-left' says it all about the wit, wisdom and intensity with which Liverpool fans regard the game. And though the human tragedies of Hillsborough and

Heysel have since reminded us that football is only a game, the players who've pulled the red shirt with the liver bird badge over their heads have always commanded the greatest respect and the most loyal support.

That's not to say that anything but 100 per cent effort will be tolerated. This may be the era of the foreign 'mercenary', when players from all corners of the globe have been attracted to play in the Premiership, but any player looking for an easy ride would be on the first train out of Lime Street. While the occasional foreigner like South African Berry Nieuwenhuys was taken to the Kop's collective heart, recent years have seen the likes of Jan Molby (Denmark) and Stig Inge Bjornebye (Norway) become firm favourites. The jury is still out on Patrik Berger, the Czech signed after Euro '96 who seemed to play half-games as often as not.

Right: Liverpool parade the European Cup, a trophy they won four times between 1977 and 1984.

Bill Shankly's teams always had more than a fair sprinkling of Scots, reflecting his own roots and the belief that you could buy well and wisely north of the border for less than in England. He also found gems in the lower leagues, like Keegan and Clemence, but there has always been a home-grown presence in Liverpool sides that's represented today by the likes of Robbie Fowler and Steve McManaman.

This book aims to cover a cross-section of the greats of today and yesterday. We can't and indeed don't claim to have covered everyone eligible, not in exhaustive detail, but the intention is to put today's Anfield idols in a context with some of the great players who've preceded them onto that hallowed turf.

It's fascinating that many have found niches in the media: Alan Hansen has proved as classy a performer on Match Of The Day as he was in 600-plus games in red, while Mark Lawrenson and Jim Beglin have both enjoyed stints as radio summarisers. Most bizarrely of all, Michael Robinson, a player who featured just 30 times in a Liverpool League shirt, has become the Des Lynam of Spain, and being fluent in the language has carved himself quite a career as Espana's Mr Football.

Most ironically of all, perhaps, is the fact that manager Roy Evans played just 11 times before hanging up his boots and turning to coaching. He may not be a Liverpool All-Time Great, unlike his predecessors Dalglish and Souness, but he still has time to make his mark as a manager.

Which of the players we feature here would make his all-time XI is another question. But we hope he, like you, will be stirred to pick your own dream team from the players who've made Anfield history.

Top: Signed from Coventry, Scottish stopper Gary Gillespie played over 150 League games for Liverpool between 1983 and 1990.

7

Liverpool Club History

The sign over the players' tunnel leading to the pitch reminds all and sundry that 'This is Anfield'. And, with the massed choir of the Kop booming out its hymn of praise to those in red and constructive criticism of those of other persuasions, it's been as good as a goal start in many cases.

Throughout their history, Liverpool FC have always had the advantage of playing at Anfield. Indeed, it's been a hard ground to take anything away from since long before the Shankly era made it an impregnable fortress, where six points dropped a season was tantamount to treason. Yet when it staged its first competitive matches back in 1888, Anfield was home to rivals Everton, who quit in 1892 after a row with the landlord, John Houlding.

ANFIELD

Having a ground and no one to play on it, Houlding decided to form his own club. Liverpool FC started from scratch, yet within a year had won elevation to the Second Division of the Football League in place of Bootle. Having obtained promotion, the first of many League Championships was won in 1900-01 when they pipped mighty Sunderland to the title after a last-game win. Their first Cup Final, in 1914, met with defeat by a single goal to Burnley, and it wouldn't be until 1950 that they'd reach the Final again.

League titles had followed in 1906, 1922, 1923 and 1947, and only a single season in the (then) Division Two in 1904-05 marred their record as top-flight ever-presents. Stars of this period included fearless keeper Elisha Scott, skilful striker Albert Stubbins and flying winger Billy Liddell, who'd serve from 1946 to 1960.

The Reds' second Cup Final saw them journey south to Wembley, to meet capital club Arsenal. Future manager Bob Paisley had scored on the run-in but was dropped for the Final itself, a rare moment of disappointment for a very successful character. Defeat by 2-0 at Wembley in 1950 was followed by relegation four years later, and a decade-long spell in the shadow of Everton. But the arrival of pocket-size Scot Bill Shankly from Huddersfield in December 1959 changed all that.

PLAYER'S CIGARETTES.

G. HODGSON. LIVERPOOL

CHURCHMAN'S CIGARETTES

W. FAGAN (LIVERPOOL)

WILLS'S CIGARETTES

B. NIEUWENHUYS (LIVERPOOL)

GOING FOR THE LEAGUE TITLE

Building round a nucleus of fellow Scots in Tommy Lawrence, Ron Yeats and Ian St John, he instilled a will to win into the side the like of which they'd never known before. Allied to the skill of England internationals like Hunt, and Thompson, the workrate of Ian Callaghan and the hard tackling of Tommy Smith, it was a recipe for success. Top-flight football returned to Anfield in 1962, the League title arrived two years later after a 17-year gap and the FA Cup finally made its way north in 1965. Don Revie's Leeds were defeated in extra time, but over the coming years would prove a constant thorn in Shankly's side.

Liverpool had ventured into Europe as Champions, but it was the Cup Winners' Cup that brought them their first taste of glory. They reached the Final in Glasgow, having beaten Juventus and Celtic en route, but Germany's Borussia Dortmund took the honours 2-1 in extra time. This wasn't the last European competition would see of the mighty Reds.

Bill Shankly's visionary style of management included buying when his side was strong and replacing key players not with panic purchases but players who'd learned the Anfield way throughout an apprenticeship in the reserve side. A larger squad was becoming necessary, too, for

Opposite: Kop heroes of years past – free-scoring Gordon Hodgson (left), wily Scot Billy Fagan (centre) and pre-war favourite Berry Nieuwenhuys.

Above: The sign over the tunnel says it all.

Above left: John Barnes takes on Everton in the 1989 Cup Final.

Left: Putting the finishing touches to an all-seater Anfield.

9

1967-68 saw Liverpool contesting the League Cup, a competition they'd traditionally considered an irrelevance. A total of 59 games that season proved that success required strength in depth.

Ray Clemence had arrived, and would eventually oust Tommy Lawrence in goal after his eight years in possession. Hunt, St John and Yeats would depart too as, after a shock 1-0 defeat at Second Division Watford, Shanks wielded the axe. It must have hurt him to take his great team apart, but compassion wins nothing in football and the names of Larry Lloyd, Steve Heighway, Alec Lindsay and John Toshack would soon be sung by the Kop with no little fervour.

There was something to sing about, too, as the Reds played their way to Wembley in 1971's FA Cup competition to set up a repeat of the 1950 Final against Arsenal. Sadly, the Cup would stay in the south again, forming part of the Gunners' glorious Double which Liverpool would emulate in 1986. Defeat in extra time was a choker, but at least it was to a superb Charlie George goal that's since been replayed as one of the

fixture's best: no blame could be attached to Ray Clemence.

The season of 1971-72 saw the name of Keegan on the team sheet for the very first time. It might also have seen Liverpool's name on the Championship trophy once more had they not endured an horrific five-game scoreless run over Christmas and the New Year. This effectively ruled them out of contention – until they assembled an equally amazing sequence of 13 wins, two draws and no defeats to appear alongside Leeds and Derby at the top of the table.

A mathematical conundrum would see the title decided while Brian Clough's Derby, who'd finished their fixtures, were sunning themselves on a Mediterranean beach. If Liverpool or Leeds could win their last game, with the other losing, they could take the prize, but although Leeds lost the Reds, away at Arsenal, failed to score and a draw was simply not good enough. John Toshack had an offside goal disallowed, further causing the third-placed Merseysiders to rue their lack of Christmas cheer.

Silverware was finally obtained in 1973 when they again faced German opposition in a two-legged UEFA

Below: Bob Paisley, Bill Shankly's successor, and the team that took the 1983 Milk Cup, beating rivals Manchester United.

Cup Final. Borussia Monchengladbach wilted in the face of the Anfield onslaught and a 3-0 home lead proved enough to take the trophy with a 3-2 aggregate. Liverpool's European record of 21 consecutive seasons from 1964-65 to 1984-85 – when it was ended by the Heysel tragedy – is indeed an enviable one.

Kevin Keegan, who scored twice in the 1973 Final, was one of Shankly's best ever buys, forming the backbone of the side that would prove as successful in the 1970s as his Cup winners had been in the 1960s. With goalkeeper Ray Clemence, a fellow England international when at Anfield, he'd been spotted playing for Scunthorpe United and brought to serve an apprenticeship in the reserves before coming through to make an impact in the first team.

The team of '73 emulated Hunt, St John, Lawrence and Yeats, who had won the League title in 1966, but, as

mentioned, went one better by adding a European trophy to the League crown. The common factor between the sides was long-serving Ian Callaghan, a winger who'd establish a club League appearance record of 640 games between 1960 and 1978.

By contrast, reserve left-back Roy Evans was allowed just two appearances that season, but would reappear later in an off-pitch role. A second FA Cup win came in 1974 against Newcastle.

Bill Shankly announced his retirement just as he unveiled Liverpool's record buy, £200,000 Ray Kennedy, to the press in July that year. Shanks was a footballing legend, even in the blue half of the city, and his death in 1981 would be widely mourned. His replacement, Bob Paisley, was unknown outside Liverpool when he took the job, but would push Liverpool to even greater heights by eclipsing Shankly's trophy haul.

Left: The Liverpool
team that beat Spurs
1-0 in the 1982
FA Charity Shield.
Back row, left to right:
Thompson, Rush,
Grobbelaar, Hansen,
Whelan, Lawrenson,
Dalglish.
Front row: Neal,
A Kennedy, Hodgson,
Lee, Souness.

Paisley rejuvenated Shankly's team by integrating the likes of Alan Kennedy and Terry McDermott, both from FA Cup opponents Newcastle and future England stars, alongside Merseysider Jimmy Case and ever-inspirational captain Emlyn Hughes. The title was claimed in 1976, and proved the key to the biggest prize of all, the European Cup. Borussia Monchengladbach were beaten 3-1 in Rome, while the Reds also retained the Championship at home. The season of 1976-77 had offered the chance of a unique 'Treble' – League, FA Cup and European Cup – but defeat by Manchester United, the previous year's runners-up, in the Final, derailed that dream.

The capture of Kenny Dalglish from Glasgow Celtic for a club record £440,000 sweetened the pill of Kevin Keegan's decision to leave English football for Hamburg. Against all the expectations, King Kenny would make just as big a mark on Merseyside as player and, later, manager. The face of the team was changing as the likes of Alan Hansen and David Johnson took over from veterans Tommy Smith and John Toshack.

Brian Clough, who'd already proved he had the Indian sign on the Reds when Derby took the title in 1972, did it again in 1977-78 with his new club Nottingham Forest who, by winning the League and beating the Reds in the League Cup Final, showed they were a new force in the land. Nevertheless, European Cup success was sweet, and inevitably it was Dalglish who scored the only goal of that game against Belgian Champions Bruges at Wembley. No British team had ever before managed to retain the European Cup, and that included rivals Manchester United.

The Championship was achieved in 1978-79 with the loss of just four games, underlining goalkeeper Ray Clemence's credentials for the England job he had to share with the equally gifted Peter Shilton. Ironically, Shilton's club Forest were put in their place by an eight-point margin, Ray keeping a clean sheet in an amazing 27 games, only four of which were lost.

The title would be retained in 1979-80, if hardly as impressively. It wasn't until January that the Reds, now without Emlyn Hughes, hit the front of the pack but they made no mistake. International class had been added at the back in Crazy Horse's stead in the substantial shapes of the two Alans, Hansen and Kennedy. A promising young Dublin-born reserve midfielder, Ronnie Whelan, also took his first steps onto Anfield's hallowed turf during the course of the season and would soon have the opportunity to make a name for himself.

THE ELUSIVE TROPHY

The League Cup had always remained elusive, but when Liverpool won it in 1981 it stayed in the Anfield trophy room for four years! The European Cup was also something of a fixture, the third win in five years coming thanks to a late goal from full-back Alan Kennedy in 1981. Their opponents Real Madrid had won the trophy six times in its early years: Liverpool were surely their 1980s equivalents.

Ray Clemence's surprise departure to Spurs at the start of the 1981-82 season made way for 24-year-old Bruce Grobbelaar, the clown prince of keepers who would become a legend over the next decade. Up front was another new name, Ian Rush – a young Welshman who just couldn't stop scoring goals. He too would write his name into Anfield history with two spells at the club, interrupted only by an unsuccessful period in Italy.

Grobbelaar's first Anfield campaign would be attended by success on two fronts, the League being accompanied by a League Cup win against his predecessor's new club, Tottenham. Liverpool's habit of playing to the final whistle stood them in good stead when, after equalising the Londoners' single goal in the 88th minute, they continued pressing and emerged clear winners through goals by the multi-national strike force of Whelan (Eire), Johnston (South Africa) and Rush (Wales)

Bob Paisley won his last trophy in May 1983, as Liverpool retained the League title by an impressive 11-point margin over Watford. The season had begun spectacularly as Leeds' record of avoiding defeat in their first 29 games, set in 1974, was equalled...typically, the team to thwart them was Everton. Even so, it was clear from the outset that the title was Anfield-bound.

Three European Cups, six League titles, three Milk (League) Cups and a UEFA Cup had made Bob uniquely successful, and the respect in which he was held was clear when he became the first manager ever to lead his side up Wembley's 39 steps to receive the League Cup that March. Their beaten opponents were Manchester United, victims of yet another dynamic 'come from behind' act.

Always quiet and unruffled even in times of stress, Paisley's nine-year reign had begun with few fanfares, but against the odds had resulted in even more honours for the club than under his outspoken predecessor Bill Shankly. Continuity had brought a rich reward: he'd been on the coaching staff since the mid 1950s, and the success of promotion from within would influence future appointments. His connection with the club continued as he took a place on the board: he died in February 1996 and was much mourned.

Joe Fagan, an Anfield boot-room regular since 1958, was Paisley's successor. Not only did he succeed in securing a third successive Championship – only Huddersfield and Arsenal having previously achieved the feat – but went one better than Paisley by adding the Milk

Above: Eire international Ronnie Whelan enjoyed a successful 15-year period at Anfield before moving to Southend where he became player-manager.

and European Cups in a unique Treble. Scots midfielder Graeme Souness, a 350-game veteran who never, ever admitted defeat, was his captain courageous, but the player's departure for Italy helped make 1984-85 the first trophyless season in living memory. Even sadder was the crowd violence at the Heysel Stadium, Brussels, that saw many lives lost before the start of the European Cup Final. Juventus prevented a second successive European Cup win, and a European ban ensured there'd be no chance to bounce back the following season.

The new manager charged with lifting morale was an old face – Kenny Dalglish, who continued his on-pitch role and crowned his first season in charge with only the third League and FA Cup Double this century. Ian Rush had progressed to prove himself one of the country's most lethal marksmen, and scored two of the Reds' three Wembley goals against Everton.

Rush finished 1986-87 as top scorer for the fifth time in six seasons, but Liverpool won nothing. He took his talents to Italian giants Juventus, but returned after a season that saw Liverpool Champions again. John

Aldridge, the man who replaced him, had made history in an unfortunate way with the first ever Cup Final penalty miss at Wembley, a single Wimbledon goal thwarting a second Double.

As Dalglish stepped down from playing regularly, he welcomed John Barnes, the first black player to be transferred to Liverpool, and Peter Beardsley, a nippy attacker who arrived from Newcastle. Both would make their mark with country as well as club.

The 1988-89 season brought a tragedy that put even Heysel in perspective when 96 Liverpool fans lost their lives at Hillsborough before a Cup semi-final against Nottingham Forest. It made a mockery of the saying attributed to Bill Shankly that 'football's not a matter of life and death…it's more important than that.' The game was eventually played at Old Trafford, but both that win and the dramatic 3-2 extra-time Cup Final triumph over Everton were occasions where thoughts were very much elsewhere. Arsenal came to Anfield needing to win by two clear goals and succeeded, depriving the Reds of another Double.

The following season saw no mistake made with the League, as they took their 18th Championship with a nine-point lead over nearest challengers Aston Villa. Ronnie Whelan, the Eire international midfielder, celebrated his tenth season as a Red, but Liverpool's third successive FA Cup semi-final ended in defeat by Crystal Palace. For the third season running they'd come close to repeating the Double triumph of 1986 only to fall in sight of glory.

Dalglish's last season in charge, 1990-91, began with ten consecutive wins and ended in a string of defeats. A light in the darkness was Jamie Redknapp, son of West Ham boss Harry, who was signed for £350,000 after just 13 League games for Bournemouth. Alan Hansen, now approaching the veteran stage, would retire at the end of the season after 600-plus games in the Number 6 shirt.

But the shock departure of the season was that of manager Dalglish, who announced his decision on 22 February 1991 after a dramatic 4-4 FA Cup draw with Everton. The strain was too much, and 14 glorious years at Anfield as player and manager were brought to an end in minutes.

The reasons for Dalglish's decision could, some theorised, be traced back to the death in 1985 of Jock Stein – his former manager and father figure with both Celtic and Scotland – while at a World Cup qualifying game at Cardiff. He'd had the results of a lifetime of stresses and strains spelled out to him on that fateful day, and when he said in his departure press conference that 'The pressure is incredible…on matchdays I just feel as if my head is exploding,' Stein must surely have been in his thoughts.

There had also been the aftermath of Hillsborough to deal with, and that had certainly extracted a price from this fundamentally decent character. Yet later he'd suggest that, had Liverpool kept his job open for him, he might possibly have returned after a much-needed sabbatical.

Significantly, in his future appointments he'd share the burden with coaches who could leap up and down from the bench and share the burden of command.

Dalglish would return to the game that October as boss of Blackburn Rovers. But with Liverpool just three points off the League leadership, the directors couldn't leave the ship without a skipper. Their choice was Dalglish's 1980s team-mate Graeme Souness, now manager of Glasgow Rangers.

THE SOUNESS YEARS

Souness set about rebuilding the team in his own competitive image, the imposing defender Neil Ruddock epitomising the never-say-die spirit. Forest midfielder Nigel Clough (the son of Brian) added class, but proved fitful. Only Mark Wright at the heart of the defence and, eventually, keeper David James would prove long-term successes. The biggest impact had come from a player who rose through the ranks – Robbie Fowler, a teenager who burst onto the scene early in 1993-94 with all five goals in a Coca-Cola Cup demolition of Fulham. He slotted in alongside veteran Ian Rush and was clearly one for the future.

Despite a massive turnover of players, the near three-year spell under Souness brought only one honour: the FA Cup in 1992. Liverpool had reached Wembley in style, beating Ipswich, Aston Villa and Portsmouth before a 2-0 win over Second Division Sunderland in a comparatively unmemorable match.

Graeme Souness's second full season at the helm started with great expectations but saw them finish just sixth. Chairman David Moores confirmed his position for a further three years in a May press conference, but at the same time appointed boot-room veteran Roy Evans as assistant manager. It was a shrewd move, and something of an insurance policy. When the forthcoming season fell apart in early 1994, the heir apparent would be at hand.

Souness would go on to managerial posts with Fenerbahce in Turkey and Southampton before quitting the Dell in 1997, having kept the Saints in the Premiership, complaining of lack of finance for team-building. He'd return to Italy with Serie B Torino. At Anfield, he'd tried to change too much too soon, ruthlessly imposing his own competitive stamp on the team – and while the tactic had worked like a dream at Rangers, where he'd won the Treble in his first season, Liverpool were up against less forgiving opposition.

Yet if one man summed up the history of Liverpool Football Club's first century, it was and would always remain Bill Shankly. The shadow he cast across the club history was no less imposing than that of fellow Scot Matt Busby at Old Trafford – yet fortunately, given the continuing glories under Bob Paisley, the memories were never a substitute for success.

The Shankly Gates, opened to celebrate the ground's 1990s redevelopment, commemorate the man in a very permanent way, the message across the top 'You'll never walk alone' taken from the lyrics of the Rodgers and Hammerstein show tune the Kop had made their own. Reputedly, Shankly had once signed a hotel register while abroad as 'occupation: football, address: Anfield'. On being told he had to fill in where he lived, he addressed the receptionist thus: 'Lady, in Liverpool there is only one address that matters – and *that* is where I live.'

Below: The Anfield boot-room in action – Kenny Dalglish, Roy Evans and Ronnie Moran.

The Club Today

The Roy Evans era began in mid-season with Graeme Souness's resignation – and the former defender could do no better than take the Reds to eighth, their lowest League position since their return to the top flight under Shankly in 1963. The environment of Merseyside football was changing, and with Everton still very much in the doldrums, the big rivalry was now not so much with the boys in blue across Stanley Park, but the club along the East Lancs Road at Old Trafford. Unfortunately, Manchester United chose 1993-94 as the year they first achieved the Double, and the magnitude of Evans' task in catching up was clear.

The team Evans inherited was listless and demoralised, having failed to react positively to their manager's motivation. Indeed, the programme for the Cup replay against Bristol City, a 1-0 loss and Souness's final match in charge, had contained a public apology from John Barnes after he had put his name to a piece in a Sunday paper that criticised the Scot's 'abrasive manner'.

Roy received a two and a half-year contract on 31 January, he approached his task with deliberation. He knew the players he was working with and resisted any panic buying. Bruce Grobbelaar was injured at Leeds, and never regained his place. An old and a new face, Ron Whelan and Robbie Fowler, returned to the teamsheet, while Michael Thomas, who'd found first-team action hard to come by, edged his way back into the picture. The combative Julian Dicks would return to West Ham, a Souness-style player who didn't fit Evans' future plans.

The season wasn't one to look back on with any happiness. Yet had one match been won it's possible a better finish could have been achieved. Having hit 13th place in early-season freefall, Liverpool had been sixth when Manchester United arrived at Anfield in late March. The visitors' 1-0 win, shaky though it was, effectively put the brake on progress for the rest of the season, and the last nine games brought just two wins and a draw.

Right: Roy Evans' appointment as manager in early 1994 steadied the Anfield ship after Graeme Souness' turbulent reign.

Opposite: Signed by Souness, David James made the goalkeeping job his own under Evans.

Anfield was also changing its face in the wake of Hillsborough, as the recommendations of the Taylor Report spelled the end of the standing terraces. The bulldozers moved in to prepare the Kop for all-seater status after the last home game against Norwich on 30 April 1994. Yet there were few, if any, dissenting voices from a community still stunned by the events of 1989.

Roy Evans' first full season in charge, 1994-95, saw him stamp his own personality on the team. Souness had bought David James from Watford, but the giant keeper had yet to make the first-team spot his own. Under Evans, he established himself as an ever-present, growing in confidence to become a real contender for full England honours which he received in 1997.

Defenders to arrive included Stig Inge Bjornebye, a Norwegian international, and John Scales, a £3.5 million buy from Wimbledon, who supplied ball-playing qualities at the back alongside the rugged ex-Spur Neil Ruddock. Phil Babb's performance for the Republic of Ireland in the summer 1994 World Cup meant Coventry could ask, and

get, £3.6 million for him. Evans now had a team he was happy with.

Crystal Palace were thrashed 6-1 in the opening game, and, when Robbie Fowler established a Premiership record against the Gunners with a hat-trick in just four minutes and 33 seconds, it looked like this could be their year. But a 2-0 defeat at Old Trafford saw things put into perspective. Everton, who'd limped along under Mike Walker, recalled one of their former players, Joe Royle, to take the managerial reins just in time to enjoy a win against Liverpool in the first derby of the season.

Everyone on Merseyside hoped the fixture would be repeated in the FA Cup Final, with both Liverpool and Everton kept apart in the Sixth Round draw. But though the Reds were sunk by German striker Jürgen Klinsmann, they had much to look forward to in their Coca-Cola Cup Final place. First Division promotion hopefuls Bolton Wanderers were no match for the rampant Reds on the lush Wembley turf. A goal in each half for Steve McManaman rendered Andy Thompson's spectacular consolation goal meaningless –

though the Trotters would return eight weeks later to beat Reading in the play-offs. On song for Wanderers throughout 1994-95 was Eire international midfielder Jason McAteer, a man would become a familiar sight at Anfield the following season after a £4.5 million transfer.

LOCAL PRIDE

With the Coca-Cola Cup in their grasp, the Reds were still chasing Blackburn Rovers and Manchester United at the top – and though they'd be unsuccessful, they beat their Lancashire rivals at home to secure local pride. Blackburn themselves arrived at Anfield in the last match of the season with Kenny Dalglish at the helm, and an emotional occasion ended in a 2-1 win for Liverpool. Home fans rejoiced with their former boss when it became clear that United's failure to win at West Ham had given 'King Kenny' the title – importantly, without any hint of favouritism on the field.

Fourth place was a significant improvement on the previous season and would have guaranteed a European spot even if the League Cup hadn't been secured. A settled team undoubtedly helped with 11 players, no less, registering 30-plus games, including ever-present David James. A young Irish winger, Mark Kennedy, was added from Millwall late in the season to add width to the attack.

Roy Evans splashed out in the summer for Stan Collymore, a much-travelled striker with a thunderbolt shot who'd scored everywhere he played: fans of Crystal Palace, Southend and Nottingham Forest had acclaimed him as a favourite, and, with a goal every two games played, he seemed value for money even at a record £8.5 million.

Stan the Man made his mark in his very first game with the winner against Sheffield Wednesday, and his threat to Robbie Fowler's place in the attack alongside Ian Rush motivated the youngster to score four against Bolton and stay on the teamsheet to the end of the season.

But November brought poor weather and poorer form as the Reds slipped to eighth. Liverpool's Coca-Cola Cup run also ended with defeat by Premiership leaders Newcastle, while European ambitions in the UEFA Cup ended at the hands of Danes Brondby thanks to a single away goal.

April brought Newcastle United and manager Kevin Keegan to Anfield for a seven-goal, see-saw thriller with a last-minute winner that saw everyone on their feet. Jamie Redknapp, who had been injured with England, was

Below: Stan Collymore's two seasons at Anfield proved hit and miss affairs, and his transfer to Aston Villa in the summer of 1997 saw Liverpool take a £1.5 million loss on their investment.

Above: England international Robbie Fowler, pictured with Ian Rush, the man from whom he learnt so much.

welcomed back just before the end of the season. It gave him the chance not only to prove his fitness for the European Championships but also, more urgently, to stake a claim in Liverpool's side for the the FA Cup Final.

Liverpool's path to the Wembley showcase had seen them vanquish the likes of Charlton, Leeds and Aston Villa en route to a mouthwatering meeting with Manchester United. But a match that promised so much failed to deliver, the teams cancelling each other out for most of the 90 minutes. Then, with extra time looming, Eric Cantona scored his 19th goal of the season in the 85th minute to give United their second Double and leave Liverpool so near yet so far.

For any other club, European qualification for the second year running, a top three League position and the FA Cup Final would be success beyond wildest dreams –

but they only expect the best at Anfield. And while this was Roy Evans' most successful year to date a trophy would have been the icing on the cake.

He went shopping again, signing Czech international Patrik Berger from Borussia Dortmund. The player had starred in the Euro '96 Final against Germany, scoring the opener from the penalty spot, but would play no more than a bit-part role in the season to come, completing few matches and coming on as substitute just as often. Ian Rush, who accepted that at 34 he could no longer be a first-choice striker, moved on to Leeds on a free transfer with Liverpool's thanks.

On an international level, 1996-97 would see new England boss Glenn Hoddle bring Dominic Matteo into his squad, along with Fowler, Collymore, McManaman and, eventually, David James. All would gain invaluable experience in the Reds' Cup Winners' Cup campaign which started against Finland's MyPa-47 and would encompass wins against Sion (Switzerland), and SK Brann (Norway) before a high-profile semi-final against holders Paris St Germain.

Things started well on the domestic front, the Reds staying unbeaten until their ninth game and notching five against Ruud Gullit's highly-rated Chelsea team of foreign superstars. That said, the opening game had seen Middlesbrough's Ravanelli hit a hat-trick before being pegged back, so perhaps the defence wasn't as watertight as had been thought.

Robbie Fowler scored four as Middlesbrough wilted 5-1 in the December return, at which point the Reds looked handily placed for a title challenge, tucked in with Newcastle behind Manchester United. And it was in March when Newcastle visited Anfield that they seemed to be making a break for it: just as the previous year, the match ended 4-3 in Liverpool's favour as the balance swung wildly between the teams. McManaman, Berger and Fowler (2) completed a great day for Kopites, but not so happy for

Kenny Dalglish who, two months earlier, had succeeded Kevin Keegan in the Newcastle hot seat just as he once had in Liverpool's Number 7 shirt.

If Europe had almost seen them seize success, domestic Cup challenges from Anfield were relatively weak in 1996-97. In both cases the club was knocked out by future Finalists: Chelsea eliminated them from the FA Cup at Stamford Bridge while Middlesbrough did likewise at the Riverside in the Coca-Cola.

League honours still seemed possible as the season reached its climax, but that longed-for European Final – the first for 12 years – was not to be. Paris St Germain scored three without reply at the Parc des Princes, leaving the Reds too much leeway to make up at home. Fowler scored early in the game, but the French defended in depth and it wasn't until Mark Wright's 80th-minute intervention that set up a torrid final ten minutes, that they looked as if they believed they could truly do it.

The season had turned into something of a nightmare for keeper David James, whose uncertainty and lack of confidence was shared by his defence. The player, who

Left: John Barnes' decade at Anfield saw him rise to club captain as he dropped back to play the midfield anchor role.

23

Above:
Jason McAteer's credentials as an Eire international were not harmed by a 1995 transfer from Bolton Wanderers.

base – to Aston Villa for £7 million. One candidate for his place alongside Robbie Fowler was Michael Owen, a teenager who came through to score his first first-team goal when he came on as sub against Wimbledon.

Owen and Matthew Carragher, a talented midfielder signed from Wigan who so far had played only on Premiership game (in which he scored), both starred for England Under-21s in their summer 1997 tournament in Malaysia. Along with several other promising youngsters, they suggested the youth system that had proved so prolific in past years was still a source of potential match-winners.

Robbie Fowler and Steve McManaman both took a break after a long, hard season and missed the summer's Tournoi tournament on medical advice, much to the distress of national coach Glenn Hoddle.

Meanwhile, Dominic Matteo, unhappy that Hoddle had not seen fit to employ him in Le Tournoi, issued a 'pick me' plea to Scotland boss Craig Brown. The talented young defender who had been born north of the border in Dumfries seemed willing to 'do a Mark Lawrenson' and leave the England reckoning through choice. Whoever he played for at international level, much would be expected of him in a red shirt in the months to come.

Another name that might loom large in 1997-98 is Bjorn Tore Kvarme, a Norwegian bought from the same Rosenborg side that gave Liverpool Bjornebye. He'd already brought a calm assurance to the right side of Liverpool's back three, allowing Jason McAteer to advance in the wing-back role he'd been given. Bjornebye had been most people's player of the year, having come into his own in his fifth season at Anfield, while Mark Wright had impressed everyone by keeping Babb, Ruddock and Scales (who'd be transferred to Spurs) out of the side.

With Fowler and McManaman sitting it out through injury problems, the summer of 1997 saw Liverpool represented by Jamie Redknapp as England prepared to contest the post-season Le Tournoi in France. But he sustained a broken leg to add to the injuries that had sidelined him the previous campaign, leaving him with a summer battle for fitness. (More happily, the press announced his engagement to pop singer Louise.)

As other clubs, notably Arsenal, wielded their chequebooks, Evans played a waiting game. The first signing to be announced was that of Norwegian international midfielder Oyvind Leonhardsen from Wimbledon, while efforts were being made to entice Italian striker Fabrizio Ravanelli to Anfield in a tug of war with local rivals Everton, now under a third spell of management by Howard Kendall.

John Barnes' future seemed less certain than ever before during his decade at Anfield, as Roy Evans left his captain out of the side for the last three matches. It seemed certain there would be major surgery as the manager attempted to keep the Anfield men at the forefront of the Premiership chase in the coming season. Because that, as ever, was the Liverpool way.

won his first full England cap during the season, had blamed his poor performances on too much video game playing, and certainly any personal collection of TV highlights from the season would have to concentrate on the early part. Yet Roy Evans persevered with him, and believed he would come good again.

Though Manchester United faltered late on, Liverpool couldn't make up the ground and indeed – after a win, a loss and a draw in May – subsided to a disappointing fourth place. Though UEFA Cup qualification was a certainty, there was an undercurrent of unrest among some sections of the support, suggesting that Roy Evans was too much the nice guy and that a steelier character might have obtained more from the players.

Evans reacted immediately the season ended, selling Stan Collymore — whose transfer had never really worked, due to inconsistent form, lack of application and his unwillingness to move to Merseyside from his Midlands

Player Profiles

GOALKEEPERS
Ray Clemence, Bruce Grobbelaar,
Tommy Lawrence.

DEFENDERS
Stig Inge Bjornebye, Alan Hansen, Emlyn Hughes,
Rob Jones, Alan Kennedy, Chris Lawler,
Mark Lawrenson, Phil Neal, Steve Nicol,
Tommy Smith, Phil Thompson, Mark Wright.

MIDFIELDERS
John Barnes, Ian Callaghan, Jimmy Case,
Steve Heighway, Ray Houghton, Craig Johnston,
Ray Kennedy, Terry McDermott, Steve McMahon,
Steve McManaman, Jan Molby, Jamie Redknapp,
Graeme Souness, John Wark, Ronnie Whelan.

STRIKERS
John Aldridge, Peter Beardsley, Kenny Dalglish,
Robbie Fowler, Roger Hunt, Kevin Keegan,
Billy Liddell, Ian Rush, Ian St John, John Toshack.

We all know how to pick a Fantasy Football team – but when Bill Shankly, Bob Paisley and Kenny Dalglish put silverware in the Anfield trophy room their achievements were real. The players signed by those three magnificent managers make up the majority of the players profiled here, along with the cream of today's stars aiming to reinstate Liverpool at the top of the English football tree.

Nearly all the players we feature are internationals, their skills as highly prized by country as well as club. There are captains of England like Hughes and Keegan, but also players like Smith and Hansen who by rights should have made more of a mark on the world stage. For a Liverpool player, though, the approval of the Kop is everything – any further accolades merely a bonus.

So turn the page and select from the choicest squad of players ever to wear the liver bird on their chest. The haircuts may have dated in some cases, but their skills and dedication are undoubted.

John Aldridge

PERSONAL FILE

Born: 18 September 1958
Birthplace: Liverpool
Height: 5' 11"
Weight: 12st 3lb

LEAGUE RECORD

FROM-TO	CLUB	APPS	GOALS
1979-84	Newport Co	170	69
1984-87	Oxford Utd	114	72
1987-89	Liverpool	83	50
1989-91	Real Sociedad	56	32
1991-97	Tranmere R	228	133
Total		651	356

LIVERPOOL LEAGUE DEBUT

21 February 1987 v Aston Villa

EIRE DEBUT

26 March 1986 v Wales

EIRE HONOURS
(TO 31 MAY 1997)

SEASON	CAPS
1985-86	4
1986-87	8
1987-88	6
1988-89	7
1989-90	10
1990-91	4
1991-92	8
1992-93	7
1993-94	6
1994-95	4
1995-96	4
1996-97	1
Total	69

DID YOU KNOW?

On returning to Merseyside, 'Aldo' set a Tranmere scoring record with a 40-goal first season.

As fellow Liverpudlian Paul McCartney would put it, it was a long and winding road for John Aldridge that led to Anfield, the ground where he'd watched his football as a youth. And, having reached soccer mecca, he prospered only to fall from favour on the return of prodigal son Ian Rush from Serie A exile. He then enjoyed two seasons in Spain before returning to spark a revival on the other side of the Mersey.

In between times he became one of Jack Charlton's adopted Irishmen, gracing two World Cups. But the tale started in Wales, at now-defunct Newport County, which offered him his first taste of League football. Next stop was Oxford, where he did manager Jim Smith proud, consistently bettering a 1 in 2 ratio and starring in the League Cup-winning run of 1986 – though, surprisingly, he didn't score in the Final.

Wembley showcases seemed to disagree with him: a penalty miss against Wimbledon proved costly in 1988 as Liverpool slumped to a single-goal defeat, though he shrugged it off to continue his superb League form in 1988-89 in tandem with Peter Beardsley, before Rush returned as first choice.

Experience with Eire helped Aldridge settle in Spain for his seasons there, and he remained an international regular. International goals had initially proved hard to come by (just one in his first four seasons in a green shirt), but he starred in the team that made the quarter-finals in Italia '90. Four years later in the States he was more often used as a substitute, as Jack Charlton's 'one-up' formation saw room for him or Quinn – not both.

At Tranmere he was an instant hit, scoring a club record 40 goals in all competitions in his first season, 1991-92, and quashing speculation that a quarter of a million pounds was too much for a 32-year-old. His strike power pushed Rovers to three consecutive promotion campaigns, all sadly unsuccessful.

Taking over from John King as manager in April 1996, he continued his scoring streak, 1996-97 yielding 18 goals in 43 League appearances as Rovers finished 11th. Should his team improve on that, it isn't impossible he might one day re-cross the Mersey to visit Anfield again, on a temporary or possibly permanent basis.

Eight of John's first ten appearances for Liverpool were as substitute despite scoring in both the games he started.

27

John Barnes

PERSONAL FILE

Born: 7 November 1963
Birthplace: Jamaica
Height: 5' 11"
Weight: 12st 7lb

LEAGUE RECORD

FROM-TO	CLUB	APPS	GOALS
1981-87	Watford	233	65
1987-97	Liverpool	314	84
Total		547	149

LIVERPOOL LEAGUE DEBUT

15 August 1987 v Arsenal

ENGLAND DEBUT

28 May 1983 v Northern Ireland

ENGLAND HONOURS

SEASON	CAPS
1982-83	4
1983-84	8
1984-85	11
1985-86	5
1986-87	3
1987-88	11
1988-89	5
1989-90	11
1990-91	7
1991-92	2
1992-93	6
1993-94	—
1994-95	5
1995-96	1
Total	79

STAR QUOTE

'I would love the chance to manage Liverpool.'

On his day, there can be little doubt that John Barnes has been one of the supreme talents to grace the post-war game in England. Nurtured by Graham Taylor during Watford's dramatic ascent through the divisions, he drove the Hertfordshire club to the 1984 FA Cup Final, single-handedly destroying Birmingham City in the quarter-finals of the competition. Although Watford were beaten by Everton at Wembley, Barnes had done enough to establish himself as one of the outstanding prospects in the country and a natural choice for England.

In one of his early games for the national side, Barnes scored an individual goal that has been described as the best ever seen in Brazil's Maracana Stadium. A solo effort that cannot be diminished – however often it is viewed – it made his eventual departure from humble Vicarage Road inevitable. Thus it was that Barnes made the trip north to Anfield, a £900,000 cheque making the opposite journey.

As Barnes joined Dalglish's army of big-money buys, some critics voiced doubts over the deal. Despite his stunning display at the Maracana, Barnes had been a profound disappointment in most of his displays in a white shirt: would he similarly struggle on the big stage at Anfield?

Such negative voices were soon silenced, for in his early years at the club no player could claim to

generate such consistent excitement as Barnes. This marriage of excellence and reliability would make Barnes the lynchpin of a side that has frequently been in a state of flux in recent seasons.

Though no longer the tormentor of full-backs, a more mature Barnes has moved inside to anchor the midfield, a task he has performed admirably as Liverpool have sought to build a base from which to challenge Manchester United's recent hegemony.

Two Championships, an FA Cup and League Cup winner's medals have come Barnes' way during his stint at the club, as has continued international recognition. But while he may boast a collection of more than 70 caps, perhaps Barnes' greatest regret will be his failure to replicate the club form that elevated him to the status of a Kop idol.

'As you get older you become more aware
of your team responsibilities...they wanted
me to play the holding role.'

Peter Beardsley

PERSONAL FILE

Born: 18 January 1961
Birthplace: Newcastle
Height: 5' 8"
Weight: 11st 7lb

LEAGUE RECORD

FROM-TO	CLUB	APPS	GOALS
1979-82	Carlisle Utd	104	22
1982	Vancouver W'caps	22	7
1982-83	Manchester Utd	—	—
1983	Vancouver W'caps	25	8
1983-87	Newcastle Utd	147	61
1987-91	Liverpool	131	46
1991-93	Everton	81	25
1993-97	Newcastle Utd	129	46
Total		639	215

LIVERPOOL LEAGUE DEBUT

15 August 1987 v Arsenal

ENGLAND DEBUT

29 January 1986 v Egypt

ENGLAND HONOURS

SEASON	CAPS
1985-86	9
1986-87	6
1987-88	11
1988-89	8
1989-90	11
1990-91	4
1991-92	—
1992-93	—
1993-94	3
1994-95	5
1995-96	2
Total	59

STAR QUOTE

'When I left Liverpool, everyone thought I was on the way out and finished...I always think I've got three or four years left.'

Rarely can a footballer of international renown have blossomed from such an unpromising beginning as Peter Beardsley. Despite impressing with Carlisle United in his early years, the best move Beardsley could secure was to Vancouver Whitecaps in Canada, playing alongside the likes of veterans Terry Yorath and Peter Lorimer.

Ultimately, Ron Atkinson ended his exile in one of soccer's backwoods, bringing him to Manchester United. But after just one League Cup appearance against Bournemouth, Beardsley found himself on the way out of Old Trafford en route to an uncertain future and another spell in Vancouver. It was only when he was picked up by boyhood favourites Newcastle United that Beardsley finally made the impression his talents merited. Playing alongside Keegan and Waddle in Newcastle's promotion-winning side, he rocketed into the national spotlight.

At the 1986 World Cup, Beardsley emerged as the natural foil for Gary Lineker, and cemented his place in the England side. As Newcastle's promise foundered, Kenny Dalglish pounced, taking Beardsley to Anfield in 1987, paying £1.8 million, a record fee between two domestic clubs.

In 1987-88, few opposing fans could chant 'what a waste of money', for Beardsley delivered the goods and the goals. His high-octane performances won plaudits from the critics and the hearts of Liverpool fans. Yet that faith did not ultimately extend to Kenny Dalglish, who chose to omit Beardsley on numerous occasions in the following seasons. His

successor, Graeme Souness, gave Beardsley even shorter shrift, selling him to Everton for £1 million in August 1991. It seemed a curious and ignominious end for a man who had bagged 46 League goals in 131 games in the famous red shirt, collecting two League Championship medals and an FA Cup winner's medal in the process.

Beardsley went on to prove he was far from over the hill with both Everton and, more recently, Newcastle, where he now had to convince Kenny Dalglish of his claim to a first-team place at 36.

Stig Inge Bjornebye

PERSONAL FILE

Born: 11 December 1969
Birthplace: Rosenborg, Norway
Height: 5' 10"
Weight: 11st 9lb

LEAGUE RECORD

FROM-TO	CLUB	APPS	GOALS
1992-97	Liverpool	90	2

LIVERPOOL LEAGUE DEBUT

19 December 1992 v Coventry City

NORWAY HONOURS

Had been capped 43 times by his country up to the start of the 1996-97 season

When Liverpool travelled to Norway for a tour prior to the 1992-93 season, Stig Inge Bjornebye could scarcely have realised the impact it would have upon his career. Already capped by his country, Bjornebye was perhaps the outstanding member of the Rosenborg side who played Liverpool that summer. A composed defender, comfortable in possession, Bjornebye caught the eye of Graeme Souness, who made a note of the talented youngster's abilities. And before the year was out, Liverpool's indifferent League form prompted Souness to make his move, the 23-year-old arriving for the comparatively modest fee of £600,000.

Bjornebye had few doubts about the move to England, for Liverpool were – and remain – the best-supported club in Norway. Plunged straight into the side, Bjornebye made a confident start, only to lose his form and his place as Liverpool stuttered towards sixth place in the Premier League. While this was no worse than the previous season, Liverpool fans had to look back to the mid-1960s for a less promising League finish. As crisis continued to engulf embattled boss Souness, Bjornebye was left on the sidelines at precisely the time the defence needed his cool head most of all.

When the board finally ran out of patience with Souness, Bjornebye found himself restored to the side, and demonstrated he had lost none of his edge. Unfortunately, disappointment lurked just around the corner, a broken leg curtailing his return to favour. Nonetheless, his phlegmatic qualities stood him in good stead and Bjornebye fought his way back to play a significant part in the 1996-97 campaign.

At only 27, Bjornebye should be running into the best form of his career, and manager Roy Evans will be looking to his reliability and versatility as Liverpool attempt to wrest the title from Manchester United in 1997-98.

STAR QUOTE

'To bounce back from a broken leg wasn't too hard...but getting back into the side was.'

Ian Callaghan

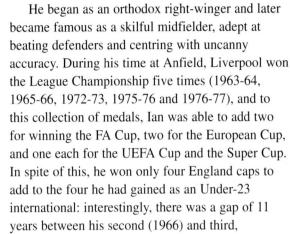

PERSONAL FILE

Born: 10 April 1942
Birthplace: Liverpool
Height: 5' 7"
Weight: 11st 1lb

LEAGUE RECORD

FROM-TO	CLUB	APPS	GOALS
1960-78	Liverpool	640	50
1978	Fort Lauderdale	20	—
1978-80	Swansea C	76	1
1981-82	Crewe Alex	15	—
Total		751	51

LIVERPOOL LEAGUE DEBUT

16 April 1960 v Bristol Rovers

ENGLAND DEBUT

26 June 1966 v Finland

ENGLAND HONOURS

SEASON	CAPS
1965-66	2
1966-67	—
1967-68	—
1968-69	—
1969-70	—
1970-71	—
1971-72	—
1972-73	—
1973-74	—
1974-75	—
1975-76	—
1976-77	—
1977-78	2
Total	4

DID YOU KNOW?

Ian Callaghan played his first Liverpool game as a replacement for Billy Liddell, yet went on to outlast even that great Kop favourite as a first-team regular.

Ian Callaghan made his first-team debut for Liverpool while the club was still in the Second Division of the Football League. A Liverpudlian by birth, he signed on at Anfield as an apprentice and never had any doubt that he would, in time, make it into the League side. His first chance came in the 1959-60 season. Liverpool were to finish third in Division Two, missing out on promotion by just one place, and would repeat this achievement the following season. By the time promotion was finally won at the end of the 1961-62 campaign, Ian Callaghan had become a very good footballer.

He began as an orthodox right-winger and later became famous as a skilful midfielder, adept at beating defenders and centring with uncanny accuracy. During his time at Anfield, Liverpool won the League Championship five times (1963-64, 1965-66, 1972-73, 1975-76 and 1976-77), and to this collection of medals, Ian was able to add two for winning the FA Cup, two for the European Cup, and one each for the UEFA Cup and the Super Cup. In spite of this, he won only four England caps to add to the four he had gained as an Under-23 international: interestingly, there was a gap of 11 years between his second (1966) and third, testimony to his continued form and fitness.

Ever-present in the Number 7 shirt, moving to Number 11 when his wing partner Peter Thompson moved on in 1973, Ian Callaghan was not only the link between Shankly's team of the 1960s and his team of the 1970s, he survived to thrive under Bob Paisley. Everton legend and record goal ace Dixie Dean said of Callaghan and Thompson, 'If I'd had those two feeding me crosses I'd have scored 100 League goals, never mind 60!'

Between the 1959-60 and 1977-78 seasons Ian played 640 League games in a Liverpool shirt, scoring 50 goals and making many, many more. He left for Swansea in the summer of 1978, joining his old team-mate John Toshack in helping the Third Division side to a second successive promotion. He later played for Cork Hibs in the Irish Republic, before, at the age of 39, he joined Crewe Alexandra for the last 15 games of his playing career.

Jimmy Case

PERSONAL FILE

Born: 18 May 1954
Birthplace: Liverpool
Height: 5' 9"
Weight: 12st 12lb

LEAGUE RECORD

FROM-TO	CLUB	APPS	GOALS
1975-81	Liverpool	186	23
1981-85	Brighton & HA	127	10
1985-91	Southampton	215	10
1991-92	Bournemouth	40	1
1992-93	Halifax T	21	2
1993	Wrexham	4	—
1993	Darlington	1	—
1993-96	Brighton & HA	32	—
Total		626	46

LIVERPOOL LEAGUE DEBUT

26 April 1975 v Queens Park Rangers

ENGLAND DEBUT

N/A

ENGLAND HONOURS

None (Under-23 only)

DID YOU KNOW?
Case signed initially as a semi-professional, believing he should complete his apprenticeship before entering the risky world of pro football.

When Liverpool's Jimmy Case stood over a free-kick, few opponents would volunteer to stand in the wall. Famed for his ferocious shot, he was also renowned as one of the fiercest competitors in the game. Along with Tommy Smith and Graeme Souness, Case provided the touch of steel so essential to Liverpool's phenomenal success in the 1970s.

Like Steve Heighway, Case was plucked from local football, signing from non-league South Liverpool in 1973. There any similarities with Heighway end, for while the winger's game relied upon grace and close skill, combative midfielder Case built his game upon raw enthusiasm. Yet for all his tough tackling, he was not without skill. His sudden surges from the middle of the park caught many sides off balance, and when he struck one of his famous piledrivers it rarely found Row Z.

The value of his role in the side is reflected in the clutch of honours he collected; three European Cup, a UEFA Cup and four League Championship winner's medals were his reward. Though his pugnacious approach probably cost him full England recognition, Case was honoured at England Under-23 level.

He finally left the club in 1981, signing for former Liverpool star Jimmy Melia at Brighton. The club was enjoying its finest hour, and Case spent a couple more seasons at the top level, even playing against Manchester United in the 1983 FA Cup Final. He later moved down the coast to the Dell, before returning to Brighton for an ill-fated spell as manager. In mid-1997, he continued his managerial apprenticeship, taking over the reigns at Dr Martens League side Bashley.

Ray Clemence

PERSONAL FILE

Born: 5 August 1948
Birthplace: Skegness
Height: 6' 0"
Weight: 12st 9lb

LEAGUE RECORD

FROM-TO	CLUB	APPS	GOALS
1965-67	Scunthorpe Utd	48	—
1967-81	Liverpool	470	—
1981-87	Tottenham H	240	—
Total		758	—

LIVERPOOL LEAGUE DEBUT

31 January 1970 v Nottingham Forest

ENGLAND DEBUT

15 November 1972 v Wales

ENGLAND HONOURS

SEASON	CAPS
1972-73	2
1973-74	3
1974-75	7
1975-76	9
1976-77	9
1977-78	6
1978-79	7
1979-80	8
1980-81	5
1981-82	3
1982-83	1
1983-84	1
Total	61

STAR QUOTE

'Ray was always capable of starting a move from defence, and his concentration was exceptional.'
BOB PAISLEY

Ray Clemence was born in Skegness on 5 August 1948 and, for a goalkeeper who was to become one of the best in the English game, the early part of his career was less than spectacular. He first joined Notts County as a junior, but signed for Scunthorpe in August 1965. After 48 appearances for the Third Division side, he was signed by Liverpool.

Ray had to wait a long time for his first-team debut. Tommy Lawrence was still the number one choice at Anfield, and Ray did not get his chance until the 1969-70 season. He had, however, perfected his skills while playing reserve-team football, and was ready to play a major part in the Liverpool success story over the next decade.

Clemence had in fact played once for the first team in his first two years at Anfield – a League Cup tie against Swansea in which he managed to keep the first of many clean sheets while with the club. His League debut followed in early 1970, a one-off just before Liverpool's FA Cup defeat at Watford that sparked Shankly's rebuilding programme.

Playing behind one of the best organised defences in football, Ray claimed nine winner's medals – five for the League Championship, one for the FA Cup and no less than three for the European Cup. He also played for England on numerous occasions and would have won far more caps had his career not coincided with that of Peter Shilton.

Having played more than 500 games for Liverpool in all competitions, and at the age of 33 – when many footballers and even some goalkeepers are considering hanging up their boots – Clemence moved to Tottenham Hotspur. He played for Spurs until early in the 1987-88 season, making a further 240 League appearances, before eventually deciding to call it a day. Having taken his total of England appearances to 61 in a remarkably long and distinguished career, he'd take his place in Glenn Hoddle's England set-up in 1996 after spells coaching Spurs (with fellow ex-Red Doug Livermore) and managing Barnet.

*When Ray Clemence signed for Liverpool,
Scunthorpe got around £400 for every game he'd
played for them.*

Kenny Dalglish

PERSONAL FILE

Born: 4 March 1951
Birthplace: Glasgow
Height: 5' 8"
Weight: 11st 13lb

LEAGUE RECORD

FROM-TO	CLUB	APPS	GOALS
1970-77	Celtic	204	112
1977-90	Liverpool	355	118
Total		559	230

LIVERPOOL LEAGUE DEBUT

20 August 1977 v Middlesbrough

SCOTLAND DEBUT

10 November 1971 v Belgium

SCOTLAND HONOURS

SEASON	CAPS
1971-72	2
1972-73	8
1973-74	12
1974-75	9
1975-76	6
1976-77	10
1977-78	10
1978-79	8
1979-80	10
1980-81	3
1981-82	10
1982-83	2
1983-84	3
1984-85	4
1985-86	3
1986-87	2
Total	102

STAR QUOTE

'He kept Liverpool on the winning path by doing it his own way.'
BOB PAISLEY

Kenny Dalglish inherited the title 'King of the Kop' from Kevin Keegan, not long after Bob Paisley signed him from Celtic in August 1977. Born in the Dalmarnock area of Glasgow on 4 March 1951, Kenny enjoyed remarkable goalscoring success with Celtic. He had helped his side to four Scottish League titles, and had winner's medals in four Scottish Cup Finals and one Scottish League Cup Final. Although he had started by occupying a midfield position, he nevertheless scored a remarkable 112 goals in 204 League encounters.

Dalglish went on to play nearly 500 games for Liverpool, scoring on more than 160 occasions. In many ways he was the complete footballer. He had remarkable ability and instant reaction, and was very determined. He also had an unselfish attitude and was therefore an excellent team man, ideal for a well-drilled Liverpool side and very useful for the Scottish international team, for whom he made 102 appearances – a record north of the border.

During his time as a Liverpool player, Kenny Dalglish collected five League Championship medals, as well as four for the League Cup and one for the FA Cup. He also played in four European Cup Finals.

Bob Paisley saw Dalglish's withdrawn, remote off-field personality as the key to how he made the transition from player to manager with ease. 'When he put on those boots he shone like a beacon,' said Paisley, 'but off the pitch he was a loner and I don't think anyone at the club would say they knew him well. It never pays for a manager to be close friends with the players under him.'

Dalglish has never been known for his extrovert behaviour. English interviewers and supporters alike may have had some difficulty in understanding an accent which mirrored an apparently dour Glaswegian personality, but when he took over as player-manager of Liverpool in June 1985, and then proceeded to win the Double the following season, no one much cared. Kenny went on to enjoy more of the success to which he had become accustomed,

and Liverpool won two more League titles and had one more FA Cup success while he was in charge.

To everyone's surprise, Dalglish resigned his managerial post in February 1991. The stresses and strains had seemingly got to him at last, but many were also surprised when he took over at Blackburn Rovers not long afterwards. More success followed, as high-spending Blackburn gained Premiership status and everyone wondered how Kenny managed to communicate with his equally unforthcoming deputy, Ray Harford. Kenny then 'moved upstairs' before taking charge at Newcastle following the early-1997 departure of Kevin Keegan.

'I knew that if I'd scoured the world I couldn't have found a more accomplished player.'
BOB PAISLEY

1993- 1997

Robbie Fowler

PERSONAL FILE

Born: 9 April 1975
Birthplace: Liverpool
Height: 5' 10"
Weight: 12st 3lb

LEAGUE RECORD

FROM-TO	CLUB	APPS	GOALS
1993-97	Liverpool	140	83

LIVERPOOL LEAGUE DEBUT

25 September 1993 v Chelsea

ENGLAND DEBUT

27 March 1996 v Bulgaria

ENGLAND HONOURS
(TO 31 MAY 1997)

SEASON	CAPS
1995-96	5
1996-97	1
Total	6

STAR QUOTE

'Robbie's a great talent: he's willing to listen, and that's good. He's got to keep his feet on the ground though.'
ROY EVANS

Liverpool born and bred, Robbie Fowler grew up an Everton fan and, like his mentor in the Liverpool team Ian Rush, made the transition from Goodison terraces to Anfield playing staff simply because the Reds were quicker to recognise his obvious talent for scoring goals.

At the age of 18, Fowler impressed during a summer tournament for the England Under-19s and was expected to start the 1993-94 season as a regular for his club.

But it wasn't to be that easy and at the end of a barren September did the youngster get his chance, in a League Cup clash at Fulham. In the return leg Fowler scored all five in a 5-0 drubbing of the Londoners and his place was secured. He went on to score three against Southampton and finished the season with 18.

The following campaign saw Fowler paired with Rush from the start and the youngster opened his account with a hat-trick against Arsenal in the first home game. He was the club's top scorer and earned a Coca-Cola Cup winner's medal after a 2-1 win over Bolton.

In 1995-96 Fowler made way for Stan Collymore, but came back after Collymore was injured. The break sharpened his game and he went on to score four against Bolton and three against Arsenal. He pocketed a staggering 36 goals, second only to Alan Shearer, and made a long-awaited debut for England in Euro '96, coming on as substitute four times.

During 1996-97, his understanding with Collymore failed to click, prompting the latter's departure to Aston Villa in May. No matter who he may partner in future seasons, we have not seen the best of this precocious talent.

1981-1994

Bruce Grobbelaar

PERSONAL FILE

Born: 6 October 1957
Birthplace: Durban, South Africa
Height: 6' 1"
Weight: 14st 2lb

LEAGUE RECORD

FROM-TO	CLUB	APPS	GOALS
1979-80	Crewe Alex	24	1
1980	Vancouver Whitecaps	23	—
1981-94	Liverpool	440	—
1992-93	Stoke C (loan)	4	—
1994-96	Southampton	32	—
1996-97	Plymouth Arg	32	—
Total		555	1

LIVERPOOL LEAGUE DEBUT

29 August 1981 v Wolves

ZIMBABWE HONOURS

Has been capped at full level by his adopted country

DID YOU KNOW?
South African-born Bruce Grobbelaar's path to English League football was eased when it was discovered his great-grandmother had been born in St Helen's, near Merseyside.

While Ray Clemence had occasionally been prone to the odd embarrassing boob, overall he conveyed a sense of slightly dour reliability. He was by no means alone in that, for, with rare exceptions, a hang-dog demeanour was the badge of office for the British goalkeeper. Clemence's replacement at Anfield, one Bruce Grobbelaar, was to change all that.

When Grobbelaar first trotted out at Anfield in 1981, fans had little idea of the sea change that was about to overtake the home penalty area. For while the extrovert man in green might have worn his heart on his sleeve, his antics were going to put supporters' hearts in their mouths. Sudden rushes from his goal line, kamikaze lunges for crosses and an apparent desire to play as a fifth defender in the days of the flat back four, led some fans to believe they had placed a clown in goal. But while he was occasionally guilty of the odd cringe-making mistake, most wished to persevere with Grobbelaar. They had noticed that behind all the showmanship lurked a good keeper, possibly the best in the game.

Grobbelaar himself attributed his devil-may-care approach to his time in the then Rhodesian army, where the war against rebels regularly placed him in life or death situations. This apparent nervelessness was never more valuable than in 1984, when Grobbelaar faced a penalty shoot-out in the European Cup Final. It's hard to say whether his wobbly legs routine influenced the unfortunate Roma penalty takers, but the outcome was certainly the one he'd hoped for.

During his colourful spell at Anfield, Grobbelaar topped 500 games, enjoying all the major domestic honours plus that European Cup success. In 1994 he signed for Southampton, before moving on to Plymouth Argyle. Throughout his time at Anfield he was proud to represent Zimbabwe, and continues to play for his national side, as well as being involved in the coaching set up.

Alan Hansen

PERSONAL FILE

Born: 13 June 1955
Birthplace: Alloa
Height: 6' 1"
Weight: 13st 0lb

LEAGUE RECORD

FROM-TO	CLUB	APPS	GOALS
1974-77	Partick Thistle	86	6
1977-90	Liverpool	434	8
Total		520	14

LIVERPOOL LEAGUE DEBUT

24 September 1977 v Derby County

SCOTLAND DEBUT

19 May 1979 v Wales

SCOTLAND HONOURS

SEASON	CAPS
1978-79	2
1979-80	2
1980-81	3
1981-82	10
1982-83	4
1983-84	—
1984-85	1
1985-86	1
1986-87	3
Total	26

STAR QUOTE

'He's what I call a classy player. He is always willing to come forward with the ball and reads the game so well.'
BOB PAISLEY

Now one of the most respected pundits in soccer, Alan Hansen's frequently acerbic remarks cannot easily be shrugged off by any footballer unfortunate enough to have incurred his displeasure. For Hansen's views carry the weight of a man who has not only done it all in football, but done it with a degree of excellence few could hope to emulate.

After relatively humble beginnings at Partick Thistle, Hansen moved to Liverpool in 1977. At 22 years of age, he little realised he would become a stalwart of the most successful English side in history, serving Liverpool with distinction for 13 years. In the circumstances, the Hansen deal might be considered the best £100,000 any Anfield boss has spent.

By the time the 1980s dawned, Hansen was a regular fixture in the Liverpool side. Superbly balanced, he was absurdly comfortable on the ball for a centre-back. His defensive duties were discharged with an elegance and poise bordering on the aristocratic, his frequent forays forward characterised by determined grace a million miles from the bullish rushes normally associated with centre-halves in unfamiliar territory.

The arrival of Mark Lawrenson in 1981 completed the strongest central pairing the League had seen for many a year. Next to thoroughbreds Hansen and Lawrenson, Manchester United's Gary Pallister and Steve Bruce would seem very Hackney Marshes. Although the premature retirement of his partner was a blow to Hansen, he remained at Liverpool until the departure of Dalglish in 1990. By then, limited by injury and with no management aspirations, Hansen felt it was time to bow out. After more than 600 largely immaculate games, helping Liverpool to virtually every honour available, few Kopites could dispute Hansen's unique place in the club's history.

Perhaps the only real blot on Hansen's career is a ludicrously small number of caps. By far the outstanding Scottish defender of his generation, a collection of 26 caps, plus omission from the 1986 World Cup squad, is less a mystery and more a scandal.

If Scotland fans continue to ponder their inability to go beyond the opening stages of major tournaments, selection decisions such as this might prove a useful starting point.

Alan Hansen's first job at Anfield was to bulk up: he put on nearly two stone without losing any of his natural pace.

Steve Heighway

PERSONAL FILE

Born: 25 November 1947
Birthplace: Dublin
Height: 5' 11"
Weight: 11st 7lb

LEAGUE RECORD

FROM-TO	CLUB	APPS	GOALS
1970-81	Liverpool	339	50
1981	Minnesota Kicks	26	4
Total		365	54

LIVERPOOL LEAGUE DEBUT

3 October 1970 v Chelsea

EIRE DEBUT

23 September 1970 v Poland

EIRE HONOURS

SEASON	CAPS
1970-71	5
1971-72	—
1972-73	1
1973-74	—
1974-75	4
1975-76	2
1976-77	5
1977-78	3
1978-79	2
1979-80	6
1980-81	5
1981-82	1
Total	34

STAR QUOTE

'When I first saw Steve playing for Skelmersdale, I told one of our coaches here he was the best amateur footballer I'd ever seen.'
BOB PAISLEY

To older Kopites, the exploits of Steve McManaman must evoke memories of another of Liverpool's truly great wide men, Steve Heighway. Like McManaman, the prospect of Heighway tearing down the flank would bring Anfield to life, particularly as he possessed an eye for goal the youngster has yet to cultivate.

With Kevin Keegan bursting from midfield in support, and the formidable target of John Toshack to look for in the penalty area, Heighway provided the bullets for one of the most prolific and downright exciting attacks in the history of Liverpool football club. It's no coincidence that Heighway's career would span the most successful phases of Bill Shankly's and Bob Paisley's tenures.

Having graduated from Warwick University, his challenging, direct style first came to Liverpool's attention when he played for amateur side Skelmersdale United in 1970. Within a year Heighway was in the Liverpool first team, scoring in the 1971 Cup Final after just two minutes. Though no doubt devastated by the club's eventual 2-1 defeat at the hands of Double-winners Arsenal, he did not have to wait long before getting his hands on winners' medals. A fixture in the Liverpool side throughout the 1970s, Heighway collected FA Cup, Championship, UEFA and European Cup honours, as well as more than 30 caps for Eire.

He eventually left Liverpool for the North American Soccer League side Minnesota Kicks in 1981, but has since returned to Anfield to look after the youth side with another former favourite, Brian Hall. Looking back on one of the more illustrious careers in the English game, it's unlikely Heighway ever regretted abandoning his original plan to become a teacher!

Emlyn Hughes

PERSONAL FILE

Born: 28 August 1947
Birthplace: Barrow
Height: 5' 10"
Weight: 12st 6lb

LEAGUE RECORD

FROM-TO	CLUB	APPS	GOALS
1964-67	Blackpool	28	—
1967-79	Liverpool	474	35
1979-81	Wolves	58	2
1981-83	Rotherham Utd	56	6
1983	Hull C	9	—
1983	Mansfield T	—	—
1983	Swansea C	7	—
Total		632	43

LIVERPOOL LEAGUE DEBUT

4 March 1967 v Stoke City

ENGLAND DEBUT

5 November 1969 v Holland

ENGLAND HONOURS

SEASON	CAPS
1969-70	6
1970-71	5
1971-72	7
1972-73	8
1973-74	10
1974-75	4
1975-76	—
1976-77	7
1977-78	7
1978-79	5
1979-80	3
Total	62

STAR QUOTE

'Although I never particularly got on with him as a man, I had nothing but respect and admiration for him as a captain on the pitch.'
TOMMY SMITH

Emlyn Hughes arrived for a club record £65,000 from Blackpool during the 1966-67 season, the highest-ever fee for a defender at the time in Britain. The 19-year-old was far from overawed at the prospect of playing for the League Champions and went straight into the side after injuries paved the way.

The following season he switched to midfield, as Bill Shankly strove to harness his enthusiasm for the game. After rugby-tackling a Newcastle player, much to the Kop's delight, he earned the nickname 'Crazy Horse' and never looked back.

His record of achievement at Liverpool remains undisputed: two European Cups, two UEFA Cups, four Championships and one FA Cup. Hughes also gained 62 England caps and was captain of both club and country. He missed just three games in his first nine years at Anfield and dominating style made him a firm favourite with the fans.

His earliest inspiration at Anfield was Ian St John. The Scottish international developed Hughes' midfield style and taught him a tactical awareness that was to prove priceless in the pursuit of honours.

As his career at Liverpool was coming to an end, he created a formidable central defensive partnership with Phil Thompson and little passed them by in the air. He inspired those around him and this was recognised when, in 1977, he won the Player of the Year award presented by football writers.

He left Liverpool in 1979 and, after taking Wolves to League Cup glory in the following year, went on – after a brief spell as Rotherham player-manager – to bring enjoyment to millions as A Question Of Sport team captain for many years. He led by example and steered Liverpool through one of the most successful periods in their history.

Ray Houghton

PERSONAL FILE

Born: 9 January 1962
Birthplace: Glasgow
Height: 5' 7"
Weight: 10st 10lb

LEAGUE RECORD

FROM-TO	CLUB	APPS	GOALS
1980-82	West Ham Utd	—	—
1982-85	Fulham	130	16
1985-87	Oxford Utd	83	10
1987-92	Liverpool	153	28
1992-95	Aston Villa	95	6
1995-97	Crystal Palace	73	7
Total		534	67

LIVERPOOL LEAGUE DEBUT

24 October 1987 v Luton Town

EIRE DEBUT

26 March 1986 v Wales

EIRE HONOURS (TO 31 MAY 1997)

SEASON	CAPS
1985-86	4
1986-87	6
1987-88	8
1988-89	8
1989-90	8
1990-91	7
1991-92	5
1992-93	7
1993-94	9
1994-95	2
1995-96	2
1996-97	3
Total	69

STAR QUOTE

'I don't think I've ever scored a bad goal – they've all been long-range efforts or curlers.'

Malcolm Macdonald, the former Newcastle, Arsenal and England centre-forward, showed he had a keen eye for midfield talent too when he rescued Glaswegian Ray Houghton from the anonymity of West Ham reserves in 1982. Macdonald's Fulham side reaped the benefit as the fine skills of the Scotsman, a player as happy to dribble as to pass, graced their side for three seasons before Oxford United, then in the top flight, swooped to secure his services for a £150,000 fee.

His value had soared to £825,000 just two years later as Kenny Dalglish added him to Liverpool's squad. He'd play some 200 games for the Reds in all competitions, including League titles in 1988 and 1990 and FA Cups in 1989 and 1992, and in his late twenties enjoyed his playing prime at the Merseyside club in the company of such players as McMahon, Beardsley and Whelan.

But, with Steve McManaman coming through fast, Graeme Souness dispatched Houghton to Aston Villa where he linked with fellow Eire internationals as Steve Staunton (another ex-Red) and Andy Townsend to win a second League Cup (his first, in which he scored, had been at Oxford) in 1994.

He returned to the capital two years later on deadline day to join not Fulham but their south London neighbours Crystal Palace. Though he could not halt their slide out of the Premiership, his combination of experience and energy proved vital to Palace as they regained top-flight status via the 1997 play-offs.

Having elected to represent Eire, his father's country of birth, rather than his own, Houghton went on to gather over 60 caps, most under the managership of Jack Charlton. Though his finest moment, ironically, was helping Eire beat Scotland at Hampden in the European Championship qualifier in 1987, he was still around to play a key role in the 1994 World Cup Finals.

A spectacular though unprolific goalscorer with a goal every five games (Fulham fans still recall a spectacular 25-yarder at Newcastle in a televised 1982 clash), Houghton was the consummate link man who got on with his job with efficiency and style. In the summer of 1997 he became player-assistant coach of Reading.

Roger Hunt

PERSONAL FILE

Born: 20 July 1938
Birthplace: Golborne
Height: 5' 9"
Weight: 11st 10lb

LEAGUE RECORD

FROM-TO	CLUB	APPS	GOALS
1959-69	Liverpool	404	245
1969-72	Bolton Wanderers	76	24
Total		480	269

LIVERPOOL LEAGUE DEBUT

9 September 1959 v Scunthorpe United

ENGLAND DEBUT

4 April 1962 v Austria

ENGLAND HONOURS

SEASON	CAPS
1961-62	1
1962-63	1
1963-64	3
1964-65	1
1965-66	13
1966-67	5
1967-68	8
1968-69	2
Total	34

DID YOU KNOW?

Roger Hunt was all set to sign for Swindon, where he was guaranteed first-team football, but wife Pat wouldn't leave the north-west. Liverpool swooped.

Although most of the records he set for Liverpool have since been surpassed by Ian Rush, Roger Hunt remains an integral part of the Anfield dynasty. He signed for Liverpool, then managed by Phil Taylor and languishing in the Second Division, in May 1959. The arrival of Bill Shankly in his first season, 1959-60, saw Hunt develop into one of the best strikers in the game: though he possessed substantial qualities before Shankly arrived, it needed the motivational forces of the great Scot to bring them to the fore.

Not that it was all one way traffic; in that 1959-60 season, when Liverpool finished third in the Second Division behind Aston Villa and Cardiff, Hunt weighed in with 21 goals as Liverpool scored 90 throughout the season. The attack wasn't a problem, so Shankly spent his initial funds on a rock-solid defence. All fell into place with the arrival of strike partner Ian St John, and in Liverpool's promotion season of 1961-62, Hunt hit a club record 41 of Liverpool's 99 goals.

The campaign of consolidation was followed by success, as Liverpool were crowned League Champions in 1963-64 and 1965-66, FA Cup winners in 1965 (Hunt grabbed Liverpool's opening goal), runners-up in the European Cup Winners' Cup in 1966 and semi-finalists in the European Cup in 1965.

Roger Hunt made 404 League appearances with Liverpool, scoring 245 times, a record Ian Rush just failed to beat. Bill Shankly's team rebuilding brought Hunt's Anfield career to an end when he was barely 31, but he then moved to Burnden Park, Bolton, and rattled in another 24 goals in 76 League appearances.

Hunt had collected his first England cap in 1961-62, his goals in the Second Division convincing Walter Winterbottom that he could score at any level. His 34 appearances (18 goals) included a winner's medal in the 1966 World Cup, a tournament he will undoubtedly remember with pride thanks to three goals in group matches. It has often been claimed that Hunt's place was in jeopardy for the Final itself as Alf Ramsey toyed with the idea of bringing back the fit-again Jimmy Greaves, but he retained his place and played an important part in the win.

Although not a particularly speedy inside-forward, Hunt was ideally suited for Liverpool's requirements during the 1960s and formed a lethal partnership with Ian St John. An extremely modest man, Roger Hunt claimed playing alongside St John made his job easier, but he was direct and resourceful and deserved every one of the goals he netted. Upon retiring as a player, 'Sir Roger', as the fans affectionately dubbed him, went into the family haulage business.

Craig Johnston

PERSONAL FILE

Born: 8 December 1960
Birthplace: Johannesburg, South Africa
Height: 5' 8"
Weight: 10st 3lb

LEAGUE RECORD

FROM-TO	CLUB	APPS	GOALS
1978-81	Middlesbrough	64	16
1981-88	Liverpool	190	30
Total		254	46

LIVERPOOL LEAGUE DEBUT

29 August 1981 v Wolves

ENGLAND DEBUT

N/A

ENGLAND HONOURS

None (Under-21 only)

STAR QUOTE

'One match against Manchester City, Craig was flying about everywhere, and Bob Paisley took him off with 20 minutes to go because we couldn't keep up with him!'
RONNIE WHELAN

Bob Paisley signed midfielder Craig Johnston from Middlesbrough for £650,000 in 1981 and immediately dubbed him 'The Headless Chicken' because of his boundless energy and enthusiasm on the pitch.

Although committed in his contribution to the Liverpool team, Johnston did not always conform to the Anfield model and he was constantly at odds with manager Joe Fagan, who replaced Paisley at the helm.

The player described his two years under Fagan as the most frustrating time of his life, even though it was Fagan who gave him one of his best runs in the Liverpool team during his seven-year spell at the club. After being substituted during the Milk Cup Final in 1984, he walked out of the stadium, ignoring the team's presentation to the Queen.

When his contract was up at the end of the 1983-84 season, he refused to sign another until Fagan had left. Kenny Dalglish came in to replace Fagan and rebuilt the player's confidence with a deft hand, the fact that they had played alongside each other giving Dalglish an insight into Johnston's attitude to officialdom.

His finest moment in a Liverpool shirt came in the 3-1 FA Cup Final win over Everton in 1986, when he stabbed home Ian Rush's cross. Johnston quit the game two years later after another FA Cup Final appearance and returned to Australia (where he was brought up) to care for his invalid sister.

While there, his business acumen came to the fore when he developed the now widely-used Predator football boot. He is still fondly remembered on Merseyside for his cavalier approach to the game.

1991-1997

Rob Jones

PERSONAL FILE

Born: 5 November 1971
Birthplace: Wrexham
Height: 5' 8"
Weight: 11st 0lb

LEAGUE RECORD

FROM-TO	CLUB	APPS	GOALS
1988-91	Crewe Alex	75	2
1991-97	Liverpool	161	—
Total		236	2

LIVERPOOL LEAGUE DEBUT

6 October 1991 v Manchester United

ENGLAND DEBUT

19 February 1992 v France

ENGLAND HONOURS
(TO 31 MAY 1997)

SEASON	CAPS
1991-92	1
1992-93	—
1993-94	3
1994-95	4
1995-96	—
1996-97	—
Total	8

DID YOU KNOW?
When Rob broke into the Crewe Alexandra side, he was the youngest outfield player the club had ever fielded.

Rob Jones' meteoric rise to fame, following his £300,000 move to Anfield from Crewe in September 1991, was breathtaking. Boss Graeme Souness signed a few misfits, but with Jones he struck gold. The talented right-back was plunged straight into the first team, making his debut in the 0-0 draw at Manchester United, and went on four months later to earn his first England cap. Under Souness, Jones was one of the few players whose place in the side was assured.

His composed style and mature, level-headed defending impressed everyone and he was duly rewarded with an FA Cup winner's medal at the end of the season. It was a feat that eclipsed that of his grandfather Bill, who had played in a losing Liverpool side against Arsenal in 1950. Another Welsh-born Jones, Joey (no relation), had starred in the Liverpool full-back berth for three years in the mid 1970s, so Rob had not one but two namesakes to live up to. Fortunately, he proved equal to the task.

When Roy Evans replaced Souness as manager, Jones was switched to attacking wing-back, a transition he made with ease, and in 1995 picked up a League Cup winner's medal after the defeat of Bolton. The arrival of right-sided Jason McAteer from Bolton saw Jones switch to the left-back position, playing there in the FA Cup Final defeat by Manchester United in 1996.

After the Final, it was diagnosed that Jones had a fractured vertebra and he was ruled out for much of the 1996-97 season.

Despite his susceptibility to injury, Jones remains one of the most gifted right-backs in the country and his chance to recover his position at the top will surely come again.

Kevin Keegan

LEAGUE RECORD

FROM-TO	CLUB	APPS	GOALS
1968-71	Scunthorpe Utd	124	18
1971-77	Liverpool	230	68
1977-80	Hamburg	90	32
1980-82	Southampton	68	37
1982-84	Newcastle Utd	78	48
Total		590	203

LIVERPOOL LEAGUE DEBUT

14 August 1971 v Nottingham Forest

ENGLAND DEBUT

15 November 1972 v Wales

ENGLAND HONOURS

SEASON	CAPS
1972-73	2
1973-74	6
1974-75	6
1975-76	9
1976-77	9
1977-78	5
1978-79	9
1979-80	8
1980-81	3
1981-82	6
Total	63

DID YOU KNOW?
Kevin Keegan cut a pop single, 'Head Over Heels In Love', which reached the Top 40 in 1979.

Kevin Keegan played 124 League games and scored just 18 goals for Scunthorpe before Bill Shankly paid £35,000 to secure his services in May 1971. Born in Doncaster on 14 February 1951, Kevin was no more than a promising youngster when he joined Scunthorpe but, as everyone knows, things changed rapidly after his transfer to Anfield.

Kevin's Liverpool career was, by the standards of some, comparatively short. However, during his six seasons on Merseyside, he was to become an all-time favourite and establish himself firmly in the Liverpool hall of fame. Operating as a striker in tandem with the bulkier John Toshack, he scored some memorable goals, as well as impressing all with his workrate. He quickly became a key member of the England squad, playing his first game in 1972 and gaining 63 caps (21 goals). So vital was he, that his absence through injury in 1982's World Cup in Spain would be blamed for the team's inability to take the trophy.

Having netted 68 times in 230 League games – during which time he picked up two League Championships as well as FA Cup and European Cup winner's medals – he forsook England for the bright lights of Hamburg. It is a measure of the gap he left that Kenny Dalglish had to be prised from Glasgow Celtic to fill his Number 7 shirt.

While in Germany, Kevin was voted European Footballer of the Year in successive seasons and it surprised many a soccer pundit when, in July 1980, he returned to this country to play for Southampton. Having scored 37 League goals in 68 games for the Saints, he moved to Newcastle in August 1982 to help the Magpies gain promotion from Division Two. When this was achieved in the 1984 season he said goodbye to a glittering playing career and headed for the golf courses of Spain.

When the helicopter arrived to take him away from St James' Park after his last appearances, it seemed he had left the game forever. He later returned to manage Newcastle, however, but quit early in 1997 when it all became too much for him.

'Kevin was very ambitious. He knew exactly
what he wanted out of the game and worked himself
to a standstill to get it.'
BOB PAISLEY

Alan Kennedy

PERSONAL FILE

Born: 31 August 1954
Birthplace: Sunderland
Height: 5' 9"
Weight: 10st 7lb

LEAGUE RECORD

FROM-TO	CLUB	APPS	GOALS
1972-78	Newcastle Utd	158	9
1978-85	Liverpool	251	15
1987	Hartlepool Utd	5	—
1987-88	Wigan Ath	22	—
1990	Wrexham	16	—
Total		452	24

LIVERPOOL LEAGUE DEBUT

19 August 1978 v Queens Park Rangers

ENGLAND DEBUT

4 April 1984 v Northern Ireland

ENGLAND HONOURS

SEASON	CAPS
1983-84	2
Total	2

DID YOU KNOW?
Though he scored winning goals in two European Cup Finals, Alan Kennedy was a notoriously bad flyer who hated the trips to away games.

As an attacking wing-back in the Liverpool tradition, Alan Kennedy had a habit of scoring vital goals for the club he joined from Newcastle in 1978. None more so than his decider against Real Madrid in the 1981 European Cup Final in Paris. In the 84th minute, with the game poised at 1-1, Kennedy made a sudden darting run into the box and smashed the ball past the perplexed keeper Agustin.

Three years later in the same competition, he secured the Treble for Liverpool with the decisive penalty in a shoot-out with Roma in Rome. The capture of the European Cup, League Championship and League Cup led to Kennedy being selected for England by Bobby Robson that summer.

He was lauded by the Kop, who nicknamed him 'Barney Rubble' because he was everyone's favourite sidekick and regularly bailed the Reds out of trouble with his well-timed interventions. He started in the side as an out-and-out winger but, after deciding to fit the Anfield mould, switched to defence and never looked back. In 1985, however, 31-year-old Kennedy was replaced in the Liverpool side by Jim Beglin and left for his home-town club of Sunderland.

He had won every major honour, except the FA Cup, more than once and his contribution to this success should not be overlooked. He was a tough-tackling defender, but when the time came to launch a counter-attack he had the pace and eye for an opening that proved invaluable.

When with Newcastle, Kennedy had got his chance to face the Reds in the FA Cup Final back in 1974 because David Craig had broken his arm and regular left-back Frank Clark switched to the right.

He suggested in a pre-match interview that he was the equal of Tommy Smith in the 'hard-man' stakes – something he was ribbed about (remembering Liverpool won 3-0) when he arrived at Anfield four years later!

1974-1982

Ray Kennedy

PERSONAL FILE

Born: 28 July 1951
Birthplace: Seaton Delaval
Height: 5' 11"
Weight: 13st 0lb

LEAGUE RECORD

FROM-TO	CLUB	APPS	GOALS
1968-74	Arsenal	158	53
1974-82	Liverpool	275	51
1982-83	Swansea C	42	2
1983-84	Hartlepool Utd	23	3
Total		498	109

LIVERPOOL LEAGUE DEBUT

31 August 1974 v Chelsea

ENGLAND DEBUT

24 March 1976 v Wales

ENGLAND HONOURS

SEASON	CAPS
1975-76	4
1976-77	5
1977-78	2
1978-79	—
1979-80	6
Total	17

STAR QUOTE

'The current team has more skill than we had. But I don't think they have as much cunning as we had.'

Ray Kennedy has become one of the best-known ex-footballers since his days at Liverpool between 1974 and 1982. In 1985 he was diagnosed as suffering from Parkinson's Disease and has since spent his time raising public awareness of the illness and dealing with his own health and personal problems.

Few who were present at his 1991 benefit match were left unmoved as he came on to the pitch to receive an ovation from the fans that had followed his widely-publicised decline. Their respect was tinged with disbelief that this was the same man that had served Arsenal and Liverpool so well.

Kennedy arrived at Liverpool as Bill Shankly's last signing at the club, three years after achieving the Double with Arsenal in 1970-71. His form had been in the doldrums for some time before new boss Bob Paisley switched him from attack to midfield and confidence was restored.

Liverpool won the League title in 1975-76 and the likeable north-easterner went on to play a major part in the successes to come. Three European Cup winners' medals, one UEFA Cup, four further Championship titles and one League Cup were won, along with 17 caps for England, in a prolific period for Liverpool Football Club as the midfield of Souness, Case, McDermott and Kennedy swept all before them.

In 1982, he transferred to John Toshack's Swansea, but things did not work out and he left for Hartlepool before trying his hand at management abroad. After Parkinson's took a grip, Kennedy was forced to concentrate on learning to live with the illness and confine his memorable contribution to football to the history books.

Chris Lawler

PERSONAL FILE

Born: 20 October 1943
Birthplace: Liverpool
Height: 6' 0"
Weight: 12st 10lb

LEAGUE RECORD

FROM-TO	CLUB	APPS	GOALS
1960-75	Liverpool	406	41
1975-77	Portsmouth	36	—
1977-78	Stockport Co	36	3
Total		478	44

LIVERPOOL LEAGUE DEBUT

20 March 1963 v West Bromwich Albion

ENGLAND DEBUT

12 May 1971 v Malta

ENGLAND HONOURS

SEASON	CAPS
1970-71	3
1971-72	1
Total	4

DID YOU KNOW?

After serving Wigan Athletic as assistant manager, Chris Lawler was given a testimonial which brought 20,000 fans to Anfield. He rejoined Liverpool for a spell as reserve team coach.

Local lad Chris Lawler was born on 20 October 1943. Like many Liverpool boys, his burning ambition was to become a professional footballer and, as he had obvious talent, he duly joined the Reds when the time came. Competition for places in the senior side was as tough as ever, but Chris was eventually selected for his first-team debut in the 1962-63 season, and he remained a Liverpool player for another 12 years.

Chris occupied the right-back position and in certain situations operated in a role which today would be described as a wing-back. Noted for overlapping down the right flank, he created a large number of opportunities for goalscoring colleagues like John Toshack and Kevin Keegan, as well as netting 41 League goals for himself.

Lawler was unlucky to miss a moment of glory in the European Cup semi-final of 1965 against Inter Milan — the day after his wedding. No-one could understand why his strike was discounted, and as it would have resulted in a 4-1 win might well have taken the Reds to the Final.

An England Youth and Under-23 international, he also won four full caps for his country and was unlucky not to win more.

As a key defender, Chris was very effective. He was very quick for a tall man and his height gave him a commanding presence. He helped his side to become one of the finest in the land during his time at Anfield, and was a major component in Bill Shankly's overall defensive strategy.

After more than 400 appearances, Chris left Liverpool in October 1975 to play under former colleague Ian St John at Portsmouth. He played in 36 League games for the Fratton Park club before ending his career at Stockport County in the 1977-78 season.

Tommy Lawrence

PERSONAL FILE

Born: 14 May 1940
Birthplace: Dailly
Height: 5' 11"
Weight: 13st 12lb

LEAGUE RECORD

FROM-TO	CLUB	APPS	GOALS
1957-71	Liverpool	306	—
1971-74	Tranmere R	80	—
Total		386	—

LIVERPOOL LEAGUE DEBUT

27 October 1962 v West Bromwich Albion

SCOTLAND DEBUT

9 June 1963 v Eire

SCOTLAND HONOURS

SEASON	CAPS
1962-63	1
1963-64	—
1964-65	—
1965-66	—
1966-67	—
1967-68	—
1968-69	2
Total	3

STAR QUOTE

'Merseyside has always had a tradition of great keepers like Tommy, with his experience and know-how.'
IAN ST JOHN

He may not conform to the slimline profile of today's goalkeeper, but it wasn't just the bulk of Tommy Lawrence that made him difficult to beat. The 'Flying Pig', as the Kop affectionately dubbed him, proved an important third of the backbone of Bill Shankly's successful 1960s side, built as it was down the middle with fellow Scots Ron Yeats at centre-half and Ian St John at centre-forward.

A five-year apprenticeship in the A and reserve teams came to an end when Jim Furnell injured a finger and found Lawrence impossible to displace thereafter. The next seven and a half seasons would see him miss just five games, as well as picking up League Championship and FA Cup medals as Shankly's Liverpool wrote their name large on the footballing map. Ever alert to danger, Lawrence would race from his area to clear danger in the manner Bruce Grobbelaar would later turn into a trademark.

The defence behind which Tommy operated was so good that his problem was often maintaining concentration for an opposition breakaway. But even he had to laugh when Bill Shankly outlined his dream:

'Wouldn't it be great if we could put a deckchair in the middle of the goal, you sitting in it, cigar in your mouth. When the ball comes you get out, catch it and say "It's a lovely day to play football, isn't it?".' It should be explained that Liverpool had won the title and still had a couple of meaningless games to play…

Lawrence and his defence conceded just 24 goals in season 1968-69, thereby establishing a League record, and it begs the question of why he was only capped three times for his country. (Perhaps it was because Tommy, who joined the club after youth trials, never played Scottish League football.) But injury in 1970 gave understudy Ray Clemence a chance to stake his claim, and, in the face of competition from the future England international, Lawrence took the ferry cross the Mersey to Prenton Park. A further 80 games followed before he hung up his gloves, but there was no doubt that Tommy Lawrence's heart belonged to Anfield.

Mark Lawrenson

PERSONAL FILE

Born: 2 June 1957
Birthplace: Preston
Height: 6' 0'''
Weight: 11st 7lb

LEAGUE RECORD

FROM-TO	CLUB	APPS	GOALS
1974-77	Preston NE	73	2
1977-81	Brighton & HA	152	5
1981-88	Liverpool	241	11
Total		466	18

LIVERPOOL LEAGUE DEBUT

29 August 1981 v Wolves

EIRE DEBUT

24 April 1977 v Poland

EIRE HONOURS

SEASON	CAPS
1976-77	1
1977-78	3
1978-79	2
1979-80	3
1980-81	5
1981-82	2
1982-83	5
1983-84	4
1984-85	6
1985-86	3
1986-87	2
1987-88	2
Total	38

DID YOU KNOW?

Former England World Cup winner Nobby Stiles, then manager of Preston, persuaded Mark Lawrenson to change from winger to central defence.

Any assessment of Bob Paisley's managerial reign must concentrate on his dealings in the transfer market, for chief among his attributes was an ability to see gifts not apparent to mere mortals. No player better illustrates this knack than Mark Lawrenson. Born in Preston, Lawrenson launched his career with the Lancashire club before moving to Brighton.

Though never less than competent, Lawrenson had scarcely set the game alight when Paisley moved to sign him in 1981. What made the buy all the more remarkable was a club record fee of £900,000. Yet, from Lawrenson's earliest days at the club, it was clear Paisley had unearthed another gem.

A commanding presence, the newcomer slotted in seamlessly alongside Alan Hansen, providing the most formidable central defensive barrier the modern English game has seen. His speed, timing and overall ability to read a game made him a pivotal figure in the great Liverpool sides of the early 1980s. Despite collecting three League Cups,

an FA Cup, four League Championships and a European Cup, Lawrenson should have bettered even this prodigious haul. Tragically, from 1986 onwards, his career was wracked by injuries, most notably the Achilles tendon trouble which ultimately brought his playing days to a premature end.

Though Lawrenson would never admit it, he may also have reflected upon a hasty decision to opt to play for Eire above England. Nonetheless, he wore the green jersey with pride in 38 outings, though never at the level his talents deserved. The sense of unfulfilled potential that attaches itself to Lawrenson also extends to a truncated managerial career, a promising beginning at Oxford United, thwarted by clashes with the club's board, being followed by a 15-month spell at Peterborough.

Lawrenson tackled one of the most unenviable tasks in soccer during 1996-97, taking on the job of defensive coach at Newcastle United. In the summer shake-up at St James', though, he found himself surplus to requirements and was signed up by Match Of The Day.

Billy Liddell

PERSONAL FILE

Born: 10 January 1922
Birthplace: Dunfermline
Height: 5' 10"
Weight: 12st 11lb

LEAGUE RECORD

FROM-TO	CLUB	APPS	GOALS
1946-60	Liverpool	494	216

LIVERPOOL LEAGUE DEBUT

7 September 1946 v Chelsea

SCOTLAND DEBUT

19 October 1946 v Wales

SCOTLAND HONOURS

SEASON	CAPS
1946-47	2
1947-48	3
1948-49	—
1949-50	4
1950-51	4
1951-52	6
1952-53	3
1953-54	1
1954-55	4
1955-56	1
Total	28

STAR QUOTE

'I preferred playing outside-left because I could cut in and shoot from the left wing with my right foot.'
BILLY LIDDELL

The successful Liverpool dynasty started by Bill Shankly, which rightly made stars of great goalscorers like St John, Hunt, Keegan, Toshack, Dalglish and Rush, has tended to overshadow the prowess and exploits of those at the club before Shankly arrived. During the 1950s the Anfield club was little more than a sleeping giant, waiting for the right man with the right ideas to wake them up. Of course, Shankly's arrival didn't so much wake the club as turn it, and English football, upside down – and in so doing has committed previous heroes to the dim and distant past.

One of the greatest of these was undoubtedly Billy Liddell. Born in Dunfermline in 1922, 'King Billy' (as the fans dubbed him) was spotted playing for junior side Lochgelly Violet. At the end of the Second World War he went straight into the League side and remained a permanent fixture in the team until 1960, making nearly 500 League appearances.

A return of 216 goals confirms Liddell as a good goalscorer, but it was the fact that he operated as a left-winger which makes him a great one, for more often than not his prime objective was the creation of goals for others. His ability to weigh in with more than his fair share made him an idol to the fanatics on the Kop, a must for the full Scottish team and a player to be watched at all times.

Liverpool's relative lack of success during his playing career (they were relegated in 1954, and he played Second Division football thereafter) meant that the loyal Liddell won little of note from the game. The highlight came early with a League Championship medal in 1947, the same year he played for Great Britain against Europe, plus an appearance in the 1950 FA Cup Final against Arsenal. He did, however, win 28 caps for Scotland, for whom he operated as a more orthodox winger but still managed to score six goals.

Billy Liddell's art has been lost over the years, for wingers became a luxury after Alf Ramsey proved you could win the game's biggest honours without them. Yet Liverpool fans fortunate enough to have seen him play will attest that he was of the old-school; fast, direct and extremely effective. After retiring, Liddell became an accountant, having taken his exams while still playing. Winger or striker, his own statistics still add up to impressive reading.

Terry McDermott

PERSONAL FILE

Born: 8 December 1951
Birthplace: Kirkby
Height: 5' 9"
Weight: 12st 13lb

LEAGUE RECORD

FROM-TO	CLUB	APPS	GOALS
1969-73	Bury	90	8
1973-74	Newcastle Utd	56	6
1974-82	Liverpool	232	54
1982-84	Newcastle Utd	74	12
Total		452	80

LIVERPOOL LEAGUE DEBUT

16 November 1974 v Everton

ENGLAND DEBUT

7 September 1977 v Switzerland

ENGLAND HONOURS

SEASON	CAPS
1977-78	2
1978-79	3
1979-80	7
1980-81	7
1981-82	6
Total	25

DID YOU KNOW?
One of Terry McDermott's best friends at school was future world light-heavyweight boxing champion John Conteh.

When Liverpool destroyed Newcastle United 3-0 in the 1974 FA Cup Final, there was no more disappointed Magpie than Terry McDermott. His misery was compounded by the fact that he was perhaps the only Merseysider in the ground who wasn't celebrating. Yet his sadness would prove short-lived, for within six months Liverpool had swooped to bring the Kirkby-born midfielder home. His journey to Anfield may have been convoluted – taking in lowly Bury as well as Newcastle – but once on home turf he matured into one of the finest attacking midfielders ever to don a red shirt.

When a youngster at Gigg Lane, Terry had been fed on a gruesome diet of malt, cod liver oil and raw egg. As Bob Paisley later joked, 'if that was the reason he became the midfield runner he was, then I suggest the Government introduces it on the National Health!

McDermott helped ensure successive Liverpool sides would not be reliant upon strikers alone for firepower. In nine years at Anfield, he plundered 75 goals in just over 300 outings. His outstanding individual contribution to perhaps the finest club side England has produced saw him scoop a host of honours.

Twenty-five England caps came his way, as well as the honour of being named both PFA and Football Writers' Player of the Year in the same season, 1979-80. Added to three European Cup winner's medals and four League titles, it ensured the McDermott trophy cabinet was at bursting point when he returned to Newcastle United in 1982.

After subsequent spells abroad, he went back to St James' Park in 1992 as assistant manager during the Keegan revolution which saw them return to the top flight. Following Keegan's departure, McDermott remained at the club and now serves as assistant to another former Anfield favourite, Kenny Dalglish.

Steve McMahon

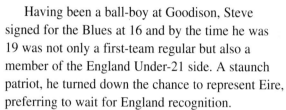

PERSONAL FILE

Born: 20 August 1961
Birthplace: Liverpool
Height: 5' 9"
Weight: 11st 8lb

LEAGUE RECORD

FROM-TO	CLUB	APPS	GOALS
1980-83	Everton	100	11
1983-85	Aston Villa	75	7
1985-91	Liverpool	204	29
1991-94	Manchester C	87	1
1994-97	Swindon T	40	—
Total		506	48

LIVERPOOL LEAGUE DEBUT

14 September 1985 v Oxford United

ENGLAND DEBUT

17 February 1988 v Israel

ENGLAND HONOURS

SEASON	CAPS
1987-88	4
1988-89	1
1989-90	11
1990-91	1
Total	17

DID YOU KNOW?
Steve turned down Anfield when he left Merseyside for the Midlands in 1983, but reconsidered two years later.

It is testimony to Steve McMahon's battling qualities that he was able to overcome the stigma of an Evertonian background to become a big hit with Kopites. Having begun his career across Stanley Park, McMahon moved to Aston Villa in 1983, where his no-nonsense approach to the art of midfield play quickly made him a favourite with Midlands fans. However, by 1985 McMahon was looking for a return north and Kenny Dalglish moved swiftly to secure his signature.

Having been a ball-boy at Goodison, Steve signed for the Blues at 16 and by the time he was 19 was not only a first-team regular but also a member of the England Under-21 side. A staunch patriot, he turned down the chance to represent Eire, preferring to wait for England recognition.

King Kenny's first signing, McMahon cost £350,000 and was bought to fulfil a very specific brief. Dalglish realised the departure of Graeme Souness had left a chasm in Liverpool's midfield, a gap that had never been properly filled.

In McMahon, Dalglish saw a man equally capable of the bonecrunching tackle or defence-splitting pass, someone who could bring bite and subtlety in equal measure (a combination sorely lacking in the present Liverpool midfield).

Playing in perhaps the last great Liverpool side, McMahon secured League Championship and FA Cup winner's medals, not to mention 17 caps for England. The great irony of McMahon's Anfield career is the fact it was curtailed by the very man he was bought to replace – Graeme Souness.

After six seasons at the club, McMahon was shipped out to Manchester City for £900,000. Since then he has carved out a promising career as a player-manager, returning Swindon Town to the First Division after it seemed the Wiltshire club was in freefall.

Steve McManaman

PERSONAL FILE

Born: 11 February 1972
Birthplace: Liverpool
Height: 6' 0"
Weight: 10st 6lb

LEAGUE RECORD

FROM-TO	CLUB	APPS	GOALS
1990-97	Liverpool	208	31

LIVERPOOL LEAGUE DEBUT

15 December 1990 v Sheffield United

ENGLAND DEBUT

16 November 1994 v Nigeria

ENGLAND HONOURS
(TO 31 MAY 1997)

SEASON	CAPS
1994-95	3
1995-96	12
1996-97	3
Total	18

If football is truly the new rock and roll, then Steve McManaman is its lead guitarist. Never afraid to go solo, the young winger is at his most dangerous when he has the ball in front of him and a full-back to torment. Born on Merseyside, McManaman's willowy build belies a powerful turn of pace, if not a powerful shot. As most Kopites will readily tell you, Jimmy Case he is not!

But if McManaman's goalscoring record is not as healthy as it might be, this does not mean he cannot produce the occasional sensational strike. His brace against Bolton in the 1995 Coca-Cola Cup Final were among the finest goals seen at Wembley in recent years. They also signified a return to form for 25-year-old McManaman who, after an impressive start, lost his way somewhat.

In recent times, however, there has been no doubting his form at club level, or his ability to please the crowd. An old-fashioned dribbler, he can both excite and frustrate, with an unrivalled ability to beat his man often let down by a poor delivery into the box. Nonetheless, he has been able to forge a potent partnership with another former apprentice, Robbie Fowler, their burgeoning understanding one of the real plus points of recent seasons.

The 1996-97 campaign saw Steve miss just one game in all competitions, scoring seven goals – equalling his best season's haul – while the previous year had brought an ever-present record. In an era when Roy Evans sought to re-establish the Red stranglehold on the title, he must have wished for a few more McManamans to give the cause added momentum.

McManaman's impressive displays have seen him deservedly claim an England place, with some critics urging boss Glenn Hoddle to give him the free role he enjoys at Liverpool. Whether Hoddle heeds these calls may well determine McManaman's international future. He has the ability to follow the likes of Matthews and Finney into the pantheon of England greats, but also the vulnerability to become the lost talent that Hoddle himself was.

STAR QUOTE

'People who say I'm one-footed are talking rubbish. To be able to run with the ball at speed you must be able to use both feet.'

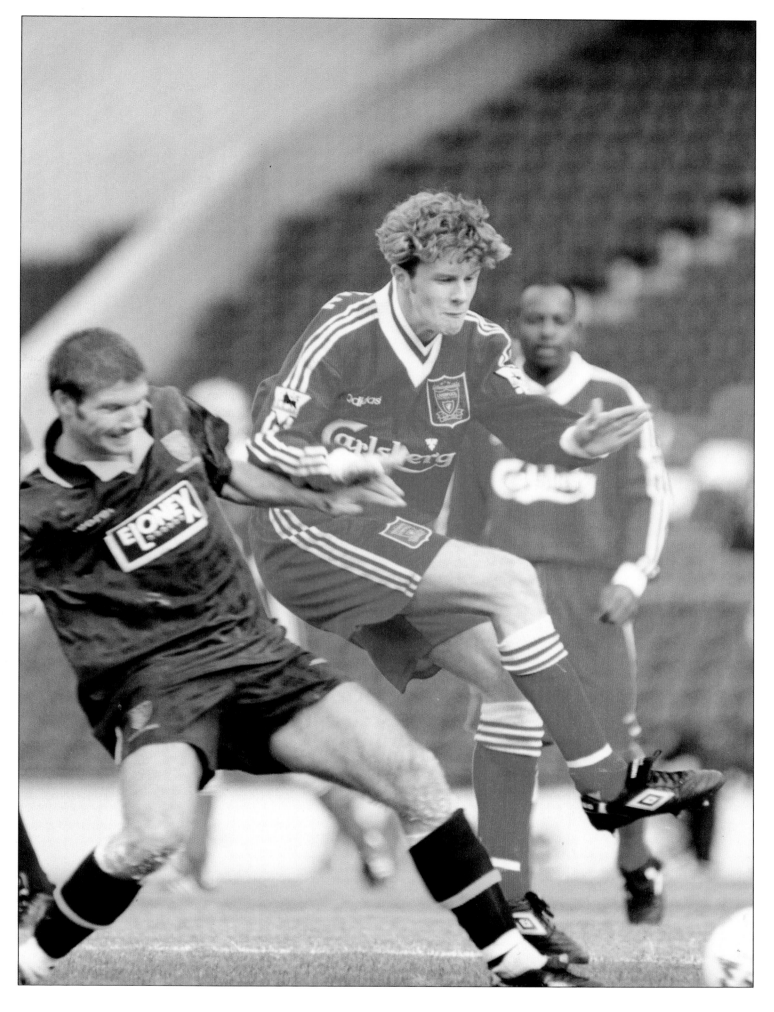

'I do love the way my club plays. I find it
harder to play for England…it's not easy.'

1984-1995

Jan Molby

PERSONAL FILE

Born: 4 July 1963
Birthplace: Kolding, Denmark
Height: 6' 1"
Weight: 14st 7lb

LEAGUE RECORD

FROM-TO	CLUB	APPS	GOALS
1984-95	Liverpool	218	44
1995	Barnsley (loan)	5	—
1995-96	Norwich C (loan)	3	—
1996-97	Swansea C	29	7
Total		255	51

LIVERPOOL LEAGUE DEBUT

25 August 1984 v Norwich City

DENMARK HONOURS

Was capped at Youth and Under-21 levels before winning 33 Danish caps during his international career

STAR QUOTE

'He became an inspiration in the heart of the Liverpool team, though at first he found it difficult to come to terms with the pace of the English game.'
PHIL NEAL

In these days when Scandinavian imports frequently fail to rise above the level of domestic journeymen, it is refreshing to recall the heyday of the finest, and certainly the most successful of their number. Signed by Joe Fagan for just £200,000 in 1984, the fact that Jan Molby arrived from Ajax offers a truer indication of his talents than the paltry fee. The Dane embodied the best traditions of total football, and would have sat happily in any midfield in Europe.

Given a level of fitness that frequently gave cause for concern, Molby's chief assets were his speed of thought and his vision. However hectic the midfield battle might be, Molby always seemed to have time, space and the ability to find the best pass available to him. Also handy in free-kick situations, Molby bagged more than 50 goals in over 230 appearances for the club and soon became a firm favourite with spectators.

This did not just spring from his footballing ability: his appearance and demeanour also won him fans. While the more earnest Kopites were exasperated by his increasingly rotund figure, others traced a linear descent from 1960s keeper Tommy Lawrence, known affectionately as the Flying Pig. Equally, Molby's unique brand of Scouse English made him one of the least remote foreign imports to ply their trade in this country.

Though frequently left on the fringes of the first team in more than a decade with the club, Molby nonetheless collected two

Championship and two FA Cup winner's medals while at Anfield. In his final season, 1995-96, he was loaned out to Norwich, among others, before eventually securing the player-manager's job at Swansea City. Though he could not prevent the Swans sliding into Division Three, in his first full season he led the club to a place in the play-offs, much to the delight of more than one Reds fan.

Phil Neal

PERSONAL FILE

Born: 20 February 1951
Birthplace: Irchester
Height: 5' 11"
Weight: 12st 2lb

LEAGUE RECORD

FROM-TO	CLUB	APPS	GOALS
1968-74	Northampton T	186	29
1974-85	Liverpool	455	41
1985-89	Bolton W	64	3
Total		705	73

LIVERPOOL LEAGUE DEBUT

16 November 1974 v Everton

ENGLAND DEBUT

24 March 1976 v Wales

ENGLAND HONOURS

SEASON	CAPS
1975-76	2
1976-77	5
1977-78	6
1978-79	7
1979-80	7
1980-81	5
1981-82	7
1982-83	10
1983-84	1
Total	50

DID YOU KNOW?
In his earlier days, Phil Neal used to job-share with Northamptonshire cricketer Peter Willey at a shoe manufacturer.

The 1960s Liverpool team had a defence that picked itself: 'Lawrence, Lawler, Byrne, Milne, Yeats…' was a litany that rolled off many a schoolkid's tongue. But when Chris Lawler bowed out in 1973, no ready-made reserve existed to fill the right-back's stylish boots. Fortunately for Bob Paisley, who inherited the problem, he bought a replacement off the peg in October 1974 in the shape of Northampton's Phil Neal.

Neal, 23, was ready for the challenge, and, after making his debut in the white heat of a Merseyside derby, proved as unflappable as they come. This would prove useful in providing Liverpool with a regular penalty-taker: given the job in 1975 after converting two in one match, it boosted his goal total over the years to a respectable one in ten games. He did likewise for England, 50 caps yielding exactly five goals.

Phil Neal was the only player to appear in all five of Liverpool's European Cup Finals, but though he seemed bound for a back-room role, was never to graduate to Anfield's boot-room. Instead, after team-mate Kenny Dalglish had beaten him to the seat vacated by Joe Fagan, he moved across Lancashire to Bolton where he'd begin his climb up the managerial ladder.

Sadly, this wouldn't prove as smooth sailing as had his playing career, and spells with Coventry, Cardiff and Manchester City all failed to bring similar success. His England record also gave him a place on Graham Taylor's staff during his turbulent reign. But Phil will always be remembered by Liverpool fans for his cultured consistency in their club's most successful period.

Steve Nicol

PERSONAL FILE

Born: 11 December 1961
Birthplace: Irvine
Height: 5' 10"
Weight: 12st 6lb

LEAGUE RECORD

FROM-TO	CLUB	APPS	GOALS
1979-81	Ayr Utd	70	7
1981-94	Liverpool	343	36
1995	Notts Co	32	2
1995-97	Sheffield Wed	42	—
Total		487	45

LIVERPOOL LEAGUE DEBUT

31 August 1982 v Birmingham City

SCOTLAND DEBUT

12 September 1984 v Yugoslavia

SCOTLAND HONOURS

SEASON	CAPS
1984-85	4
1985-86	7
1986-87	—
1987-88	6
1988-89	4
1989-90	2
1990-91	3
1991-92	1
Total	27

STAR QUOTE

'Along with Rushy, Bruce Grobbelaar and myself, Steve was the backbone of the Liverpool team through the 1980s.'
RONNIE WHELAN

Steve Nicol was plucked from obscurity at Ayr United for £300,000 in 1981 while working as a labourer to supplement his part-time football. On arrival at Anfield, he was immediately thrust into the reserves, a typical Liverpool apprenticeship that many future legends have undergone.

Coming into the team in midfield wearing Number 5, he became a regular squad member in the 1983-84 side that won the European Cup Winners' Cup in Rome. Nicol was a major player for a decade at Anfield as he went on to win a clutch of major honours, playing in every defensive position before switching back to a midfield role.

His contribution was often understated but he was an integral part of the some of the best line-ups this country has ever seen. He made his debut for Scotland in the 6-1 drubbing of Yugoslavia at Hampden in 1984 and went on to win 27 caps, the peak of which must have been the 1986 World Cup Finals, although he missed out four years later through injury.

At Anfield, he developed a fine on-field partnership with new signing John Barnes. Possibly his finest hour for the club was in scoring a hat-trick against Newcastle at St James' Park – a game in which he also had a fourth disallowed.

The fact that Steve had the biggest boots of anyone at Anfield was endlessly regurgitated in programme notes up and down the country but, as Bob Paisley observed, 'he was also one of the biggest talents.'

In 1989, he became one of the few defenders to be recognised as the PFA's Footballer of the Year. Nicol left Anfield in 1995 for Notts County but, after the Magpies were relegated, he moved on to David Pleat's Sheffield Wednesday and once more became the same solid operator he was during his Anfield days.

Jamie Redknapp

PERSONAL FILE

Born: 25 June 1973
Birthplace: Barton on Sea
Height: 6' 0"
Weight: 12st 10lb

LEAGUE RECORD

FROM-TO	CLUB	APPS	GOALS
1990-91	Bournemouth	13	—
1991-97	Liverpool	157	16
Total		170	16

LIVERPOOL LEAGUE DEBUT
7 December 1991 v Southampton

ENGLAND DEBUT
6 September 1995 v Colombia

ENGLAND HONOURS
(TO 31 MAY 1997)

SEASON	CAPS
1995-96	5
1996-97	3
Total	8

STAR QUOTE
'Liverpool came in for me, and quite honestly I wouldn't want to be at any other club in the world.'

Kenny Dalglish felt he had seen enough of Jamie Redknapp's raw talent to snap up the 17-year-old for £350,000 in 1991 from Bournemouth, after just 13 first-team appearances for the South Coast side managed by his father Harry. Redknapp took time to settle at Anfield but, with the arrival of Roy Evans at the helm, he made the central midfield position his own.

He excelled during the 1994-95 season that culminated with a League Cup winner's medal, and struck fear in the nation's defences with his prowess in dead-ball situations. One of his best was a free-kick against a Blackburn side on their way to the Premiership title.

However, in November 1995, he strained a hamstring during his third game for England and faced a four-month lay-off. He was finally recalled to the side for an FA Cup semi-final against Villa when he made the opening goal for Robbie Fowler, again from a free-kick. Displacing Michael Thomas, who had done well in his absence, he retained his position for the rest of the season and contributed to an 18-game unbeaten run for the Reds.

Redknapp has had to cope with many off-field distractions, such as his emergence as a teenage heartthrob, and is far from the finished article on the pitch. Even so Liverpool have reportedly turned down a £5 million offer from an unnamed Italian club eager to add the player to their squad, and though his seasons at Anfield have thus far been hit by injury he is clearly regarded by Roy Evans and his board as an integral part of the Red machine. Interestingly, he was Kenny Dalglish's last buy for the club a month before his resignation.

Despite Liverpool's relatively disappointing 1996-97 season, which ended in May 1997 with a broken ankle on England duty, he has time on his side and should go on to become one of the best midfielders ever seen for both club and country.

1980-1987 & 1988-1996

Ian Rush

PERSONAL FILE

Born: 20 October 1961
Birthplace: St Asaph
Height: 6' 0"
Weight: 12st 6lb

LEAGUE RECORD

FROM-TO	CLUB	APPS	GOALS
1979-80	Chester C	34	14
1980-87	Liverpool	224	139
1987-88	Juventus	29	7
1988-96	Liverpool	245	90
1996-97	Leeds United	36	3
Total		568	253

LIVERPOOL LEAGUE DEBUT

13 December 1980 v Ipswich Town

WALES DEBUT

21 May 1980 v Scotland

WALES HONOURS

SEASON	CAPS
1979-80	2
1980-81	1
1981-82	6
1982-83	4
1983-84	7
1984-85	4
1985-86	4
1986-87	4
1987-88	6
1988-89	4
1989-90	2
1990-91	7
1991-92	3
1992-93	6
1993-94	6
1994-95	5
1995-96	2
Total	73

Ian Rush's Liverpool career spanned two of the club's finest generations. He graduated from Chester City, where he had scored 14 goals in 34 League games, in 1980 and, despite the £300,000 fee, spent his first couple of seasons adapting before becoming the focal point of the side that won three consecutive Championships.

His partnership with Kenny Dalglish must rank as one of the all-time great double acts. Dalglish's ability to drop off and play the killer pass perfectly complemented Rush's searing pace and deadly finishing, and it was fitting that the two should be in tandem when Dalglish, in his first year as player-manager, helped Liverpool to their first title and FA Cup Double in 1986.

After crashing in 30 goals as Liverpool finished runners-up the next year, Rush decided to try his luck abroad, earning the club a record £2.75 million. His Anfield record stood at 139 goals in 224 League games, a phenomenal testament to his contribution to the club's greatest era.

Yet it was not over. After one year with Juventus, Rush came home. He was not an automatic choice as John Aldridge had done a superb job in his absence, and scored seven goals from 16 starts in Division One. But the triumphant return was sealed when he scored twice in the 3-2 win over Everton to lift the 1989 FA Cup.

The next season he thrashed in 18 goals in 36 games as Liverpool regained the Championship and Aldridge moved on. Another runners-up place followed (16 goals in 37 games), but times were changing at Anfield under Graeme Souness. Further FA Cup success in 1992, Rush scoring after an injury-damaged season, could not hide the fact that the Liverpool dynasty was in danger of collapsing.

With Roy Evans in charge, Rush tucked in another 12 League goals in 36 games as the side finished fourth and won the Coca-Cola Cup in 1994-95, but the grand old man of the Liverpool side could no longer be certain of his place and left for Leeds in the summer of 1996.

Yet, though the move proved less than happy, Rush was assured legendary status as Wales' record marksman, with 28 goals in 73 appearances and an all-time record of 42 FA Cup goals.

DID YOU KNOW?

Ian Rush was chased by Burnley and Wrexham as well as Chester, but felt the Turf Moor club were 'so highly organised there would be no room for a laugh.'

Ian St John

PERSONAL FILE

Born: 7 June 1938
Birthplace: Motherwell
Height: 5' 7"
Weight: 11st 6lb

LEAGUE RECORD

FROM-TO	CLUB	APPS	GOALS
1956-61	Motherwell	n/k	n/k
1961-71	Liverpool	336	95
1971-72	Coventry C	18	3
1972-73	Tranmere R	9	1
Total		363	99

LIVERPOOL LEAGUE DEBUT

19 August 1961 v Bristol Rovers

SCOTLAND DEBUT

6 May 1959 v West Germany

SCOTLAND HONOURS

SEASON	CAPS
1958-59	1
1959-60	5
1960-61	1
1961-62	6
1962-63	6
1963-64	1
1964-65	1
Total	21

DID YOU KNOW?
Ian St John played his very first representative game for Scottish Boys' Clubs with Ron Yeats, and they made their Liverpool League debuts together too.

The 'Saint' was probably the best centre-forward Liverpool has ever seen, but manager Bill Shankly had to battle to get him. The board were unwilling to fork out a club-record £37,500 for the Motherwell striker, but Shankly insisted and finally got his man.

A stylish and persistent striker that ran defences ragged as he constantly arrived at the right place at the right time to put the ball away, he struck up a formidable striking partnership with Roger Hunt and was as generous a provider as he was a ruthless finisher.

Liverpool fans still talk about the diving header he scored against Leeds at Wembley to win the 1965 FA Cup Final. In the mid-1960s St John was an integral part of Bill Shankly's great team with a front line of Callaghan, Evans, Hunt, St John and Thompson.

St John had much in common with the man that brought him to Anfield and came closest to epitomising the strength and character that Shankly sought as he built his all-conquering team. The Saint returned to Motherwell as manager in 1973 but a subsequent spell at Portsmouth was less successful.

He had his own radio show during his days at Liverpool and carried over his experience to become a widely known football pundit, following his departure from Anfield and brief stays at Coventry and Tranmere. He co-hosted The Saint And Greavsie Show on ITV and has become a natural in front of the camera.

But it was as centre-forward for Liverpool that most will remember him, his 424 appearances and 118 goals along with 21 Scotland caps and his abrasive and unswerving service during a memorable era for Liverpool Football Club.

Tommy Smith

PERSONAL FILE

Born: 5 April 1945
Birthplace: Liverpool
Height: 5' 10"
Weight: 11st 7lb

LEAGUE RECORD

FROM-TO	CLUB	APPS	GOALS
1962-78	Liverpool	467	36
1978-79	Swansea C	36	2
Total		503	38

LIVERPOOL LEAGUE DEBUT

8 May 1963 v Birmingham City

ENGLAND DEBUT

19 May 1971 v Wales

ENGLAND HONOURS

SEASON	CAPS
1970-71	1
Total	1

DID YOU KNOW?

Tommy Smith's secret superstition was to take out a couple of false teeth before every game and hand them to trainer Ronnie Moran for safe keeping until after the match.

Manager Bill Shankly wanted a hard man – and that's what he got after spotting the potential in 15-year-old Tommy Smith when signing him in 1962. Liverpool-born Smith was an uncompromising defender who had opponents quaking in their boots even before kick-off, but the self-confessed 'headcase' had a steep learning curve after making his debut at 18.

This was wonderfully illustrated in his first match against Manchester United at Anfield when experienced Scot Denis Law, annoyed at the unrelenting attention he was getting, feigned a headbutt. The Kop jeered Smith's over-reaction, leaving him humiliated.

He grew up fast and became part of a formidable unit alongside Ron Yeats, before taking the central-defensive role himself. Dubbed the 'Anfield Iron', Smith was sent off just once in his career which underlined his 'hard but fair' attitude to the game. He'd play most of his later games at Anfield in the Number 2 shirt, having moved over to make way for Hughes and Thompson.

Smith's finest moment at Liverpool was one of his last at the club. After regaining a place in the side through injury, he made his 600th appearance for Liverpool in the 1977 European Cup Final against Monchengladbach and scored a rare goal with a bullet header from the edge of the box to put Liverpool on the path to a 3-1 victory. He should have made the Final the following year but, after dropping an axe on his foot while gardening, was forced onto the sidelines.

Leaving Anfield in 1978 to join John Toshack's revolution at Swansea, Smith was part of the squad which won promotion from the Third Division. He currently commentates for Merseyside's local radio.

Graeme Souness

PERSONAL FILE

Born: 6 May 1953
Birthplace: Edinburgh
Height: 5' 11"
Weight: 12st 13lb

LEAGUE RECORD

FROM-TO	CLUB	APPS	GOALS
1970-73	Tottenham H	—	—
1973-78	Middlesbrough	176	22
1978-84	Liverpool	247	38
1984-86	Sampdoria	56	8
1986-90	Rangers	50	3
Total		529	71

LIVERPOOL LEAGUE DEBUT

14 January 1978 v West Bromwich Albion

SCOTLAND DEBUT

30 October 1974 v East Germany

SCOTLAND HONOURS

SEASON	CAPS
1974-75	3
1975-76	—
1976-77	—
1977-78	4
1978-79	5
1979-80	5
1980-81	3
1981-82	8
1982-83	9
1983-84	3
1984-85	7
1985-86	7
Total	54

STAR QUOTE

'Graeme was the strongest character I have ever met as a player, and a natural choice as our captain.'
BOB PAISLEY

Having acquired the status of a legend at any football club, it takes guts to return as manager and risk draining that reservoir of goodwill. To do it at a club the size of Liverpool is a huge gamble, and the bigger the legend, the bigger the gamble. When Kenny Dalglish spun the wheel, he emerged on top or at very least broke even. When Graeme Souness took the plunge he lost – and lost badly.

That Souness was a legend brooks no argument. After a false start at Tottenham he moved to Middlesbrough in 1973, where he formed a crucial part of Jack Charlton's promotion-winning side. Such was the impression Souness made during his five years on Teesside, that Boro fans in 1997 voted him the greatest Middlesbrough player of all time over Juninho, Pallister et al.

Yet while Boro fans no doubt harbour warm memories of that period, it was in another red shirt that Souness made his mark. Signed by Bob Paisley for £325,000 in 1978, he represented the perfect marriage of creativity and aggression, the ball-winning artist that managers up and down the country search for in vain. It's fair to say that, in the same way certain boxers claim the centre of a ring, so Souness dominated the centre of the park – and in scarcely less pugnacious style. As skipper, he was utterly committed to the cause and netted three European Cup winner's medals, five Championship medals and four League Cup winner's medals. Fifty-four Scottish caps added to a career which Souness capped in Italy, leaving Anfield for Sampdoria in 1984.

Yet to anyone who knew him, it was clear Souness was itching to try his hand at management, and when the Glasgow Rangers job was offered to him in 1986 he jumped at the chance. Radically shaking up the club, he imported experienced English stars, reversing the transfer trend of previous decades. The result was to lay the foundations of the nine successive titles Rangers fans celebrated in 1997. Souness, however, was only around for two of them. After the Dalglish departure in February 1991, his eyes were firmly on the Anfield hot seat, and his appointment rarely looked in doubt.

Upon joining the club he adopted the radical tactics he had used at Rangers, sweeping out many of the old guard, notably Beardsley, in favour of the likes of Dean Saunders and Paul Stewart. It was a bold move, a bid to solve the problem of an ageing side in one fell swoop. But Anfield, a dynasty built on evolution not revolution, was rocked to its core. Despite winning the FA Cup in 1992, poor League form and embarrassing results against lower-division opposition proved a deadly cocktail for Souness. A home FA Cup defeat by Bristol City in 1994 proved the final straw.

Undaunted, Souness went on to manage Galatasaray in Turkey and latterly Southampton, where his fighting qualities helped ensure the south coast outfit's survival for another year of Premiership football in 1997-98 – though his May resignation meant it would be without him. Instead, he received another stamp in his passport as he undertook to return Italian giants Torino to the top flight at the first attempt.

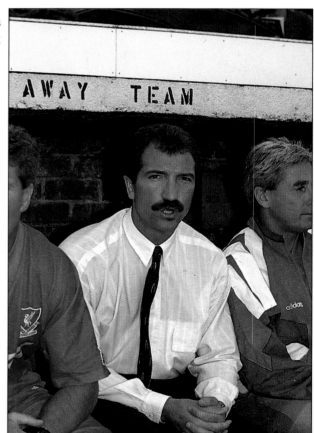

'I haven't known anybody who could
    boss a game like he could, and he always put
everything in.'
        RONNIE WHELAN

Phil Thompson

PERSONAL FILE

Born: 21 January 1954
Birthplace: Liverpool
Height: 6' 0"
Weight: 11st 8lb

LEAGUE RECORD

FROM-TO	CLUB	APPS	GOALS
1971-84	Liverpool	340	7
1984-86	Sheffield Utd	37	—
Total		377	7

LIVERPOOL LEAGUE DEBUT

3 April 1972 v Manchester United

ENGLAND DEBUT

24 March 1976 v Wales

ENGLAND HONOURS

SEASON	CAPS
1975-76	7
1976-77	1
1977-78	—
1978-79	7
1979-80	11
1980-81	3
1981-82	11
1982-83	2
Total	42

STAR QUOTE

'You would rarely see him bundled over and he had an agile brain that allowed him to read the game better than most.'
BOB PAISLEY

Phil Thompson was an outstanding central defender. Born in Liverpool, he was almost inevitably an apprentice at Anfield and signed professional forms shortly after his 17th birthday. Bill Shankly knew he had a good 'un, but Bob Paisley was to reap the benefit. Phil's first League appearance came during the 1971-72 season, and he remained at Anfield until 1984.

Though tall enough for a central defender, it took Thompson some while to fill out his six-foot frame. Bill Shankly took one look at the youngster and suggested he had tossed up with a sparrow for a pair of legs – and lost!

Liverpool won the First Division title in 1972-73, and went on to win it seven more times while he was at the club, Phil qualifying for a Championship medal for six of those campaigns. On the domestic front, he also won an FA Cup winner's medal in 1974, when Liverpool beat Newcastle 3-0 in the Final, and two League Cup winner's medals. There were European triumphs as well, Liverpool winning the European and UEFA Cups.

Thompson won England Youth and Under-23 caps, and went on to make 42 appearances in full internationals. His confidence, combined with great composure and the ability to set up goalscoring opportunities, made him a vital part of Liverpool's 1970s' success story, as well as causing him to become a very fine England player. In December 1984, with injuries having already threatened a premature end to his playing career, he decided to try his luck with Sheffield United.

Unfortunately for Phil, he was unable to carry on for very long. After just 37 games for United he was forced into early retirement at the age of 32.

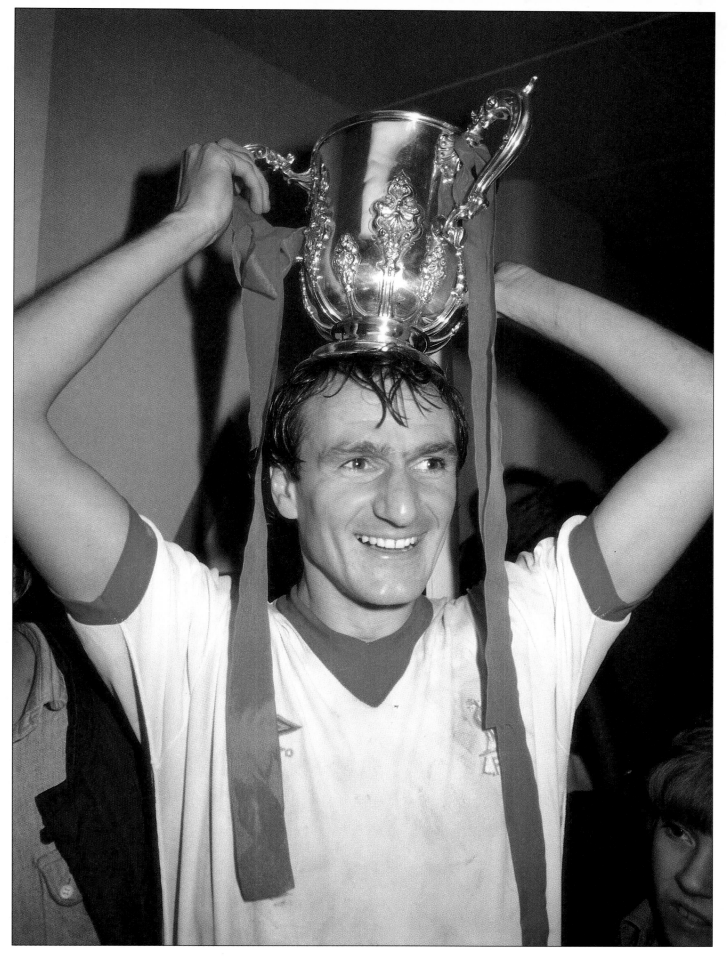

'Phil Thompson came from the same
tough Merseyside district of Kirkby
that spawned Terry McDermott.'
PHIL NEAL

John Toshack

PERSONAL FILE

Born: 22 March 1949
Birthplace: Cardiff
Height: 6' 1"
Weight: 12st 0lb

LEAGUE RECORD

FROM-TO	CLUB	APPS	GOALS
1966-70	Cardiff C	162	75
1970-78	Liverpool	172	74
1978-84	Swansea C	63	24
Total		397	173

LIVERPOOL LEAGUE DEBUT

14 November 1970 v Coventry City

WALES DEBUT

3 May 1969 v Scotland

WALES HONOURS

SEASON	CAPS
1968-69	6
1969-70	2
1970-71	4
1971-72	2
1972-73	5
1973-74	—
1974-75	7
1975-76	3
1976-77	1
1977-78	4
1978-79	5
1979-80	1
Total	40

DID YOU KNOW?

Though Bob Paisley set up a deal with Leicester that fell through on medical grounds, John Toshack fought back to regain his first-team place.

John Toshack was born in Cardiff on 22 March 1949, and was an apprentice at his local club before turning professional in March 1966. A tall and strongly built centre-forward, he made his Second Division debut during the 1965-66 season in a Cardiff side struggling to avoid relegation. Cardiff struggled quite a lot during John's early years with the club, but his total of 75 goals in 162 League appearances up until his transfer to Liverpool in November 1970 helped them maintain their Division Two status.

When Toshack signed for Liverpool he was the club's most expensive signing. The £110,000 fee may seem like the proverbial peanuts today, but at the time was a substantial investment in a footballer yet to play in the top division. John settled in well, however, and was soon knocking in the goals as the Reds strove for continued success.

An intelligent striker, he was especially good in the air and forged a tremendous partnership with fellow striker Kevin Keegan. In all, he scored 95 goals during his eight seasons at Anfield, and while he was there Liverpool won the League Championship three times, the UEFA Cup twice and the FA Cup once. John was capped by Wales on 40 occasions.

Having learned a great deal from the Anfield experience, Toshack moved to Swansea as player-manager in March 1978. He stopped playing regularly in 1980 but achieved spectacular success as manager at the Vetch Field. Swansea moved from Division Four to Division One in just four seasons, and at the end of the 1981-82 campaign found themselves in a remarkable sixth place in the top flight. Swansea's success could not last, but John later took Real Sociedad to victory in the Spanish Cup and led Real Madrid to the Spanish League Championship.

In 1997, Toshack was considered for the vacant Everton manager's post but lost out, allegedly because of his Anfield connections., Undaunted, he signed up to coach Besiktas of Turkey.

John Wark

PERSONAL FILE

Born: 4 August 1957
Birthplace: Glasgow
Height: 5' 11"
Weight: 12st 12lb

LEAGUE RECORD

FROM-TO	CLUB	APPS	GOALS
1975-84	Ipswich T	296	94
1984-88	Liverpool	70	28
1988-90	Ipswich T	89	23
1990-91	Middlesbrough	32	2
1991-97	Ipswich T	153	18
Total		640	165

LIVERPOOL LEAGUE DEBUT

31 March 1984 v Watford

SCOTLAND DEBUT

19 May 1979 v Wales

SCOTLAND HONOURS

SEASON	CAPS
1978-79	5
1979-80	4
1980-81	2
1981-82	7
1982-83	5
1983-84	5
1984-85	1
Total	29

DID YOU KNOW?

When Ipswich won the UEFA Cup in 1981, John Wark scored exactly half of his club's impressive 28-goal total, including two hat-tricks.

A tough, strong-running Glaswegian, John Wark is most closely associated with Ipswich Town, but could be said to have enjoyed his best years at Anfield. A shrewd purchase from the East Anglians, Wark cost Joe Fagan a mere £450,000. For a goalscoring midfielder at the height of his powers it represented a snip, even by 1984 standards.

Wark had already tasted FA Cup success with Ipswich and was an established Scottish international. Even more crucially, he was well acquainted with European football, having inspired Ipswich to UEFA Cup victory in 1981. His contribution was recognised by that year's PFA Player of the Year Award.

Fagan had bought the finished article, and Wark did not disappoint. Equally at home in a defensive or attacking midfield position, he proved to be the consummate professional, helping the Reds to the title in 1984. The following season he banged in 27 goals in all competitions, filling Terry McDermott's boots in midfield.

Had a broken leg not intervened in 1986, Wark may well have gone on to become the mainstay of the side for seasons to come, particularly given his subsequent durability.

But in 1988 he was allowed to return to Ipswich, supposedly a shadow of his former self. However, in a rare error of judgement, the Liverpool boot-room had reckoned without Wark's tenacity, and watched him recover sufficiently to still be playing League football at the grand old age of 39!

Ronnie Whelan

PERSONAL FILE

Born: 25 September 1961
Birthplace: Dublin
Height: 5' 9"
Weight: 12st 3lb

LEAGUE RECORD

FROM-TO	CLUB	APPS	GOALS
1981-94	Liverpool	362	46
1994-96	Southend Utd	34	1
Total		396	47

LIVERPOOL LEAGUE DEBUT

3 April 1981 v Stoke City

EIRE DEBUT

29 April 1981 v Czechoslovakia

EIRE HONOURS

SEASON	CAPS
1980-81	1
1981-82	2
1982-83	3
1983-84	1
1984-85	7
1985-86	2
1986-87	6
1987-88	7
1988-89	5
1989-90	5
1990-91	2
1991-92	1
1992-93	3
1993-94	6
1994-95	2
Total	53

DID YOU KNOW?

Ronnie Whelan was a rabid Manchester United fan, but evaded the Red Devils' scouting net to play his top-class career 30 miles down the East Lancs Road.

Bob Paisley's legendary eye for a bargain proved itself again with the purchase of Ronnie Whelan in 1979. Snapped up from Irish League side Home Farm for a nominal fee, Whelan offered Paisley the complete midfield package, with all the stamina and enthusiasm of a youngster on top of his game. Although predominantly left-sided, the key to Whelan's game was his versatility and willingness to do a job for the team. This occasionally saw him deployed at the back, where his robust tackling made him a useful stand-in.

But it was in midfield where Whelan was to make his mark. As he matured physically, his prowess as a ball winner made him increasingly valuable as he allied this to an ability to retain possession and find his man. Often the link man in Liverpool's famous lightning counter-attacks, Whelan established himself as a crucial member of the side from 1982-83.

In the following seasons, he reaped a bumper harvest of honours, including a European Cup winner's medal, six League Championship medals and two FA Cup winner's medals, not to mention three League Cup winner's medals in well over 400 games. With a healthy sprinkling of Irish caps as well, Whelan can be well satisfied with his achievements as a player.

After being dogged by injury at the tail end of his career, Whelan joined Southend United in 1994, ultimately becoming player-manager. However, with little support or resources, Whelan has seen the Shrimpers relegated from the First Division in 1996-97. And, sadly, it appeared he would need all the lessons gleaned from Paisley, Fagan, Dalglish and company to reverse the downward spiral. He quit Southend in summer 1997.

Mark Wright

PERSONAL FILE

Born: 1 August 1963
Birthplace: Dorchester
Height: 6' 2"
Weight: 13st 3lb

LEAGUE RECORD

FROM-TO	CLUB	APPS	GOALS
1980-82	Oxford Utd	10	—
1982-87	Southampton	170	7
1987-91	Derby Co	144	10
1991-97	Liverpool	152	5
Total		476	22

LIVERPOOL LEAGUE DEBUT

17 August 1991 v Oldham Athletic

ENGLAND DEBUT

2 May 1984 v Wales

ENGLAND HONOURS
(TO 31 MAY 1997)

SEASON	CAPS
1983-84	1
1984-85	7
1985-86	5
1986-87	3
1987-88	6
1988-89	—
1989-90	8
1990-91	10
1991-92	2
1992-93	1
1993-94	—
1994-95	—
1995-96	2
1996-97	—
Total	45

DID YOU KNOW?

Mark owes his break to Lawrie McMenemy, who signed him for top-flight Southampton in 1982 after just ten League appearances.

After an impressive World Cup in Italy in 1990, Mark Wright was brought to Anfield by Graeme Souness for a fee of around £2 million from Derby County – but the big centre-half initially failed to reproduce that form, despite being part of the team that lifted the FA Cup in 1992.

He suffered in the final months of Souness' reign at the club and looked jaded, to say the least, as he struggled in a side that had lost confidence due to constant personnel changes.

With the introduction of Roy Evans as manager, things started to look brighter and, despite being sent home from a pre-season tour, Wright was determined to resurrect his Anfield career. But he was out of the team and in the slow lane before seeking advice on a constantly nagging Achilles injury.

After correct diagnosis and subsequent treatment, he was back in line for a recall – and finally got it after an injury to John Scales paved the way. In the 1995-96 season, Wright was a permanent fixture in the side, finding the form that had deserted him since his arrival. He was steady as a rock in defence and quick to move the ball out into attacking areas if he saw the chance.

Confirmation of his resurrection came when England boss Terry Venables recalled him to the national side in 1996 after four years on the sidelines. His resurgence is a relief to all those who thought he was a panic buy for a crumbling regime.

Top 20 League Appearances

1	Ian Callaghan	1959-78	640
2	Billy Liddell	1946-60	494
3	Emlyn Hughes	1967-79	474
4	Ray Clemence	1967-81	470
5	Ian Rush	1980-87, 1988-96	469
6	Tommy Smith	1962-78	467
7	Phil Neal	1974-85	455
8	Bruce Grobbelaar	1981-94	440
9	Alan Hansen	1977-90	434
10	Elisha Scott	1912-34	430
11	Chris Lawler	1960-75	406
12	Roger Hunt	1959-69	404
13	Donald McKinlay	1909-29	393
14	Arthur Goddard	1901-14	388
15	Ronnie Whelan	1981-94	362
16	Gordon Hodgson	1925-36	359
17	Ron Yeats	1961-71	358
18	Alan A'Court	1952-65	355
18	Kenny Dalglish	1977-90	355
20	Ronnie Moran	1952-65	343
20	Steve Nicol	1981-94	343

Right: Goalkeeper Bruce Grobbelaar won League Cup medals in each of his first three seasons with the Reds.

League Cup Record 1968-97 – The Highs and Lows

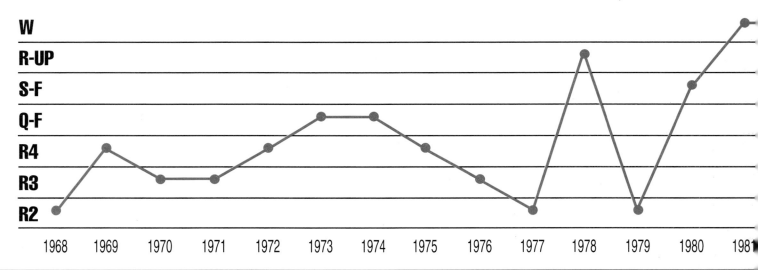

76